Helping Your Family through PTSD

Helping Your Family through PTSD

GREG E. GIFFORD

Foreword by John Babler

RESOURCE *Publications* · Eugene, Oregon

HELPING YOUR FAMILY THROUGH PTSD

Resource Publications
An Imprint of Wipf and Stock Publishers
199 W. 8th Ave., Suite 3
Eugene, OR 97401

www.wipfandstock.com

PAPERBACK ISBN: 978-1-5326-1779-9
HARDCOVER ISBN: 978-1-4982-4276-9
EBOOK ISBN: 978-1-4982-4275-2

Manufactured in the U.S.A.   JUNE 19, 2017

To Dr. Bob Somerville:
a faithful friend and fellow sufferer
who walked with me through this project.
Thank you.

To our United States Military:
I consider it an honor to have served with you.
May this book serve you.

To my wife:
thank you for lending me to this project.
I love you.

And after you have suffered a little while, the God of all grace, who has called you to his eternal glory in Christ, will himself restore, confirm, strengthen, and establish you.

—1 Peter 5:10

Contents

Foreword

GREG GIFFORD HAS BUILT upon his experience as an Army Officer as well as his training and experience as a biblical counselor to craft a very helpful overview of and biblical response to what the world calls PTSD. This book will be especially valuable to biblical counselors and family members of those suffering from PTSD. Actually, anyone who wants to understand the issues surrounding PTSD and then be better equipped to respond to those struggling with these issues will benefit from reading this book.

The world today is filled with many challenges and crises. More and more it is becoming obvious that people do not live through significant crisis and just "bounce back" to the way they were. I have been involved in the emergency services for 20 years and firefighters and police officers often struggle with recurring memories of scenes they have seen. I remember one police diver tell me that when he trains new divers on body recovery he tells them not to look at the face of the victim. He says it is something that you never forget. Sometimes these memories go beyond being something that you never forget and become prominent, haunting, and debilitating. PTSD is a label and diagnosis that can be applied to people in such situations. Greg points out that PTSD is an interpretive disorder that has God-given solutions.

By and large the church and most biblical counselors are not prepared to help people suffering with PTSD. Most are intimidated by the significance and severity of the traumas people have faced and also have a sense of inadequacy to respond. Family members of those suffering from PTSD are also at a loss to help as their loved ones frequently tell them they can't understand and they weren't there.

This book will help the reader to develop " . . . heightened awareness of the complexities of PTSD and the Scripture's robust ability to speak into those complexities." It provides suggestions for ways to provide hope, ministry ideas, and practical steps to help people deal with the issues of PTSD. In the midst of the words focused toward Biblical Counselors and family members, Greg also provides a short, but very beneficial charge and encouragement directly to those suffering with PTSD.

You may already know someone suffering from PTSD and want to understand the issue better and be better equipped to minister to him or her. You may just want to better prepare yourself to minister when you do encounter someone struggling with PTSD. In either case this book will be of great benefit to you.

John Babler, Ph.D.
Fort Worth, Texas

Acknowledgments

WE ALL STAND ON the shoulders of others in our lives. I just happen to stand on the shoulders of many godly men who have greatly influenced my life and contributed to this book. This book would not be in existence without the feedback of Dr. Bob Somerville, who worked with me to ensure I was on the right track biblically. Dr. William Varner graciously gave to make this book possible and walked me through the nuances of publication. Dr. John Street gave me the opportunity to teach biblical counseling, and Dr. Stuart Scott provided helpful input to the publication process, too. Dr. John Babler graciously allowed me to study under him, and is a personal embodiment of one ministering to those in trauma. Dr. Ernie Baker helped me understand the broad-applicability and sufficiency of the Word of God. Dr. Kevin Carson showed me that God's Word deals with the problems we face in life, something for which I will always be thankful.

As I write to families, I must acknowledge that I come from an excellent family. Doug and Mary Gifford emulate much of what I have written here. My wife, Amber, has patiently walked with me through the entirety of my Army service and through the writing of this book. She patiently endured long separations in the Army, and short ones for this book!

If this book is of any help to those facing PTSD, it is another form of God's kindness to me. "To him be glory in the church and in Christ Jesus throughout all generations, forever and ever. Amen" (Eph 3:21).

Chapter 1

Introduction

IT SEEMS LIKE YOU cannot control the memories. In the blink of an eye you are transported to the moment in your life that has in so many ways, shaped your life. Maybe it was a relationship, a car accident, a deployment; a moment in time that you would gladly pretend never existed. John felt that way. After leaving a work Christmas party last year he was involved in the worst night of his life. The memories he has—as fragmented as they are—supplement what witnesses later reported. Another car simply did not see him and pulled directly out in front of his car. John hit the other car before he hit his brakes and the driver of the other car died instantly. There was no foul play, no alcohol, not even a ticket issued. John was driving the speed limit with seat belts buckled. Yet no matter the facts, John relives that night on a daily basis. "What if I had stayed at the party longer?" he asks, or "How come I didn't leave the party when I knew I should have?" The regret and guilt perpetually hover over his life like a cloud. All it takes is a smell, a sound, or a thought to transport him back to that terrible night when he unwillingly took the life of another person.

This book aims at entering into the world of people like John, people who are sufferers. The aim of this work is to enter into the world of sufferers to enable them to see their lives as God sees their lives. It aims to equip sufferers of post-traumatic stress disorder and to show them that PTSD is an interpretive disorder that has God-given solutions. In the middle of that process not only will they be greatly helped but also God will be greatly glorified. May he see fit to use this work to bless his people!

CONTEXTUALIZING SUFFERING

It must be said, however, on the outset that this work is an attempt to contextualize suffering, both eternal and temporal suffering. Eternal suffering being that of suffering in a literal hell apart from the fellowship of God for eternity; temporal suffering in that whether for a moment or a life-time, the suffering is temporary compared to the suffering of eternity. Post-traumatic stress disorder is unequivocally suffering and one of the most terrible realities of the disorder is that it is an internal suffering. There are often no physical ailments, no diseases, and no illnesses that are swirling around PTSD but rather a plethora of emotions that people are facing. It would be unfair to shove PTSD into a category of *other than* suffering when, in fact, the very fabric of PTSD is suffering: suffering of the soul or inner man.

So to our battle stations we go. What is my mission, or rather, what is our mission? Our mission is this: to alleviate suffering, especially eternal suffering.[1] I say that eternal suffering and its prevention is our ultimate goal because it would be terrible to deliver a person from a hellish experience on earth without warning them of an infinitely worse eternity. So at the very core of our efforts to alleviate temporal suffering is an effort to alleviate eternal suffering. We set our sights on suffering and as we unravel the complexities of now, we warn of the dangers of later. We must take the sufferer to the God who created them. In that process the wise family member must determine if their loved one knows God as their Father or if they need to introduce them for the first time. They must also seek to orient the sufferer to God's purposes in their suffering and help them see how God is using their suffering

1. Piper, "Abortion and the Narrow Way that Leads to Life, "

for their good and his glory. O may we never think only of the suffering in this life! May our gaze be into eternity as we encourage and walk alongside the sufferer of PTSD.

Our desire should be to bless fellow brothers and sisters who are battling PTSD by taking them to the one who is the "man of sorrows and acquainted with grief" (Isa 53:3). He knows. And beyond knowing, he cares (Heb 4:14–16). Our ambassadorial relationship to them should seek to embody that same wise love of Christ—knowing and caring. May this work serve as a means to that end.

Ultimately, I intend to show you through this book what PTSD looks like, how to biblically respond to it, and minister to families being affected by it. As much as we would love to wipe away all suffering from the face of this globe, we know that God has planned otherwise. In fact, the crucible of suffering is often where he forms the most fruitful vessels. So we dare not circumvent that process. We dare not teach our family members that life is about comfort. We dare not stay at arms lengths from the messiness of PTSD. We dare not shirk the opportunity to minister the Gospel to people who are suffering. We must enter in to PTSD with a redemptive posture: one that says, "And after you have suffered a little while, the God of all grace, who has called you to his eternal glory in Christ, will himself restore, confirm, strengthen, and establish you. To him be the dominion forever and ever. Amen" (1 Pet 5:10–11). That is where we are going in this work: to the ones suffering with PTSD and the families ministering to them.

THE TERM "PTSD"

I am going to work with the label *post-traumatic stress disorder* because of its pre-understanding.[2] Although there could be a great

---

2. *Pre-understanding* connotes the idea that the audience has already done the difficult work of associating meaning to a term. In the context of any psychological label that can be beneficial and un-beneficial. For PTSD, it is merely a description that needs further clarification, which is where we are going in this work. It could take another volume to build a case for a more accurate description of PTSD, which I implore the reader to consider.

benefit in relabeling the phenomenon of PTSD, I default to a position as the food critic, not the chef. So let's take the term as it stands and interact with its connotations in this book. May the reader find assurance that I wish the term to be otherwise but do recognizes it as it is.

And lastly, I am acutely aware of the trend of PTSD in Western society. Having served four years as an Army officer, I saw fellow brothers in arms being told not only what they were experiencing but also how they should respond to those experiences. It was troubling at best and saddening at worst. This book is the voice of one crying in the wilderness that PTSD is the new ADD. With the demarcation lines of trauma blurring, we will see a trend over the next few years that envelopes a huge chunk of society into a group of sufferers: suffers of PTSD. May God grant us wisdom to minister wisely!

Chapter 2

Disassembling the Complexities of PTSD

"Saul has killed his thousands and David his tens of thousands"
—The Bible

A SURVEY

"Saul has killed his thousands, and David his tens of thousands" (1 Sam 18:7). This was the victory song of the women of Israel, yet it is a victory song packed with violence. Sure it was an exaggeration (which Saul did not appreciate) but it does not take long in reading the Old Testament to see that David was a man of war (cf. 1 Sam 17:36, 17:51, 18:27). He was exposed to violent animals, violent people, and combat on a regular basis. Or, in other words, he was exposed to traumatic events regularly. How has trauma shaped your life or the life of your loved one? David was exposed to some pretty rough violence—even at a young age. Maybe this is something that resonates with you? In modern terms, we would equate some of David's experiences to be *traumatic* events. Most likely, these events that could push David into a group of sufferers experiencing what has been coined post-traumatic stress disorder.

Post-traumatic stress disorder (PTSD) has begun to shape many lives across the world. To use *begun* is not to imply that it has not existed for decades past; that would be naive. The reason I have selected *begun* in this phrase is because there has been a pandemic of sorts for those affected by this terrible disorder as briefly mentioned above. Its prevalence can be attributed to a plethora of reasons, some of which we will unpack in this book. In route to that destination, we are going to look at what secular psychology would call post-traumatic stress disorder and a biblical evaluation of those conclusions.

THE STRESSOR

PTSD is often associated with an event. A moment in time where a person is directly or indirectly, singularly or repeatedly, exposed to "death, threatened death, actual or threatened serious injury, or actual or threatened sexual violence."[1] The nature of this disorder is saddening as we contemplate the atrocities to which some are exposed, sometimes, on a regular basis. This stressor can be anything from a terrorist to a parent, from a car wreck to a firefight. The intricacies of a stressor are both narrow and wide. Narrow in the sense that they can be specifically pointed to and wide in the sense that they can be a way of life for some people.

Thus, it can be deduced that to locate a stressor is not always a straightforward process. It is sometimes more of a consideration of potentialities rather than an articulation of definite causes. Compound this thought with the thought that not everyone interprets life the same way and you can have a tangled mess of real-world pain.[2] Pain that doesn't require sterile categories to articulate its existence and pain that doesn't have to be compartmentalized. Nevertheless, it is quite difficult to pin down a specific stressor and

1. United States Department of Veterans Affairs "What is PTSD."
2. See Chapter 4 for a discussion on PTSD as an interpretive disorder.

in a very real way, this is not a matter of great importance. Just because a stressor may be difficult to pinpoint does not mean that the effects of that stressor are any less real. That being said, what does PTSD look like?

THE DEFINITION

We have articulated what incites PTSD, yet we have not articulated what PTSD looks like. For many, this seems as foreign as inspecting a moon rock, while for others it is their life. For those suffering with PTSD, the following paragraphs will not be informative, they will be descriptive: descriptive of *their* life. Therefore, we must approach a definition with the same sensitivity as we should in drawing out the stressor that started this whole mess.

The National Institute for Mental Health describes PTSD as follows:

> When in danger, it's natural to feel afraid. This fear triggers many split-second changes in the body to prepare to defend against the danger or to avoid it. This "fight-or-flight" response is a healthy reaction meant to protect a person from harm. But in post-traumatic stress disorder (PTSD), this reaction is changed or damaged. People who have PTSD may feel stressed or frightened even when they're no longer in danger.[3]

Drs. Emily Rozer and Daniel Weiss state that:

> According to generally accepted criteria, diagnosis of PTSD requires exposure to a traumatic event that causes feelings of extreme fear, horror, or helplessness. Traumatic events are defined as experiences that involve death, serious injury, or threat of death. The consequences of this exposure are manifested in three symptom clusters required for diagnosis: involuntary re-experiencing of the trauma (e.g., nightmares, intrusive thoughts), avoidance of reminders and numbing of responsivity (e.g.,

3. The National Institute of Mental Health, "What is Post-traumatic Stress Disorder?"

not being able to have loving feelings), and increased arousal (e.g., difficulty sleeping or concentrating, hyper-vigilance, exaggerated startle response).[4]

There is a theme of unconscious and ongoing responses to a traumatic event that expresses itself in a negative way. Combine these definitions and you have a traumatic event that caused traumatic memory and affected biological and non-biological reactions. You have an assortment of problems and issues that now need to be addressed.

THE SYMPTOMS

The *Diagnostic and Statistical Manual of Mental Illnesses* has been the consistent pacesetter for the psychological and psychiatric field.[5] It has functioned as both a thermometer and thermostat. Some have taken what was intended to be a tool for evaluation and made it a tool for determination. While this does not negate the helpfulness of the DSM, it should stimulate the wise Christian to come with arm-length suspicion; suspicion that wants to know but does not want to be confined.

With that being said, we can begin to interact with the DSM's definition of the symptoms of PTSD. They are: (1) re-experiencing symptoms, (2) avoidance symptoms, and (3) hyper-arousal symptoms.[6] These over-arching categories help assimilate the myriad of ways that these symptoms are expressed, but their frequency must "last longer than three months, cause you great distress, and disrupt your work or home life."[7]

4. Ozer and Weiss, "Who Develops Post-traumatic Stress Disorder?," 169–72.

5. With the release of the DSM V there has been much conflict in regards to the over-diagnosing of normal human behaviors. Cf. "New Psychiatric Manual, DSM-5, Faces Criticism for Turning 'Normal' Human Problems Into Mental Illness. The rift concerning the new DSM is exposing some of the skeletons in the closet and is very clearly articulating some of the instabilities of the psychological method of diagnosis (praise the Lord!).

6. The National Institute of Mental Health, "Post-Traumatic Stress Disorder."

7. The United States Department of Veteran's Affairs, "PTSD and DSM-5."

Re-experiencing problems look like flashbacks of the traumatic event. They are horrific replays of the tragic event. Sometimes these come in the form of a nightmare and in other times it can happen while fully awake. There are circumstances that function as a trigger that takes the person back into the traumatic event that continuously haunts them. For some, this is as simple as taking a bath or falling to sleep.[8] For others, it can be a bang or backfire from a car that will incite such vivid memories. Re-experiencing problems are the intersection where the past and the present collide—sometimes repeatedly.

Avoidance symptoms take on a different look. The basic premise is that you want to avoid any and all resemblances of the traumatic event that you experienced. I knew one gentleman who served in Vietnam who would not play a modern, non-lethal alternative to combat: paintball. The memories would become too vibrant and too negative for him and it would be more helpful to just not go than to have to interact with such unpleasant circumstances. This is true for survivors of natural disasters, combat, abuse, and the myriad of other ways that trauma can affect a person. They can develop a habit of avoiding so that they can either compartmentalize those emotions or ignore, sometimes both.

Lastly, there are the symptoms of what is termed *hyper-arousal* or *hyper-agitation*. These are primarily physiological arousals that are stimulated by some type of trigger. This looks like insomnia, restlessness, being overtly sensitive to little noises, difficulty focusing, and feeling vulnerable while in public places. This is very much a physiological response to the stressor, which can seem uncontrollable at times. This symptom and re-experiencing symptoms are some of the most difficult symptoms to bear because they feel uncontrollable. It is as if the switch is turned on and there is no de-escalation or calming down.

While much research could be conducted to determine what is the chicken and what is the egg for a trigger and its physiological response, physiological symptoms are often scary and feel uncontrollable for those experiencing them. For those in the middle of

---

8. Scott and Lambert, *Counseling the Hard Cases*, 36–37.

the flashback episode, it is of little importance to determine what was the trigger but what is significant is how they can respond to the trigger. As a counselor or family, we are not afforded the privilege of such theorizing. We need to help with both the response and identifying certain triggers as we can. We want to identify triggers so as to prepare responses, not cultivate avoidance. This will be our attempt in chapter 7 as we think through biblically wise and appropriate ways to engage these physical responses. These responses are something that must be addressed if a person ever hopes to overcome the tragedies of PTSD. In light of the secular sciences evaluation of PTSD, lets take a look at what the Bible says in reference to PTSD.

A BIBLICAL EVALUATION

As briefly mentioned above, the Scriptures are full of examples of trauma. Joseph was thrown into a pit and sold into slavery (Gen 37), David is in combat before he is 20-years-old (1 Sam 17), Paul was shipwrecked (Acts 27) and nearly beaten to death (2 Cor 11:5), the disciples in the sea of Galilee almost died (Mark 4:35–41), and Jesus was crucified after being beaten in a most gruesome manner (Matt 27). These are only a glimpse of the atrocities that are mentioned in the Bible. We could spend pages talking about the rapes, pillaging, murders, battles, storms, pestilence, and other forms of trauma that have plagued human history. So there is hope for the one experiencing PTSD that the Bible *does* speak cogently into what they are suffering, or in other words, the Bible speaks into trauma. But what does the Bible *say* about PTSD? First, lets disassemble some components of PTSD from a biblical perspective.

Anxiety and Control

PTSD involves a great amount of anxiety: anxiety about both past issues and present realities. Anxiety over regrets and anxiety over potential reoccurrence of the terrible tragedy all combine for this toxic, soul-shrinking perspective on life. And thankfully, the Bible says much about anxiety.

To begin with, we must note that anxiety flows from a heart that worries and seeks to control the wrong things. Control-issues manifest themselves in many ways. They will look to manipulate others, circumstances, health, nutrition, and a myriad of other factors. Often one thinks that a control issue means that they like their doors to be locked multiple times or their house to be spotless. While those are certain manifestations of control-themes, control can take a plethora of routes, avenues and lanes to show its ugly head.

One specific area of control is the desire to know the future, plan the future, and *control* the future. (Don't think job and personal life only, but also think worrying over when a flashback will occur or being anxious over their response to a trigger: those are control issues over future events, too.) The one with control issues will often think that if they do not do it, no one will. In regards to PTSD, one may try to control their environment, control when they may have a flashback, control all of the dynamics of this but all to their increasing level of anxiety. They can't control their environment, circumstances, and some of the potential stressors/triggers—nor should they.

If a person did not want to control a circumstance, it would not matter that the circumstance was out of their control. Yet because their circumstances and triggers are out of their control, they are anxious. Anxiety is antithetical to a life of trust in God; it could even be a form of functional atheism (1 Pet 5:7). The reason is that anxiety, at its core, says that "I know best, I must figure this out, *I need to get this under control.*" When in reality, we are not even close to being in control and knowing what's best. "The fool says in his heart that there is no God" (Ps 14:1) and those with anxious thoughts (including those in the middle of a struggle with PTSD) have to saturate their life with doctrine of the presence of God (Ps 139).

The presence of God is said to be one of the most calming and energizing doctrines in Scripture. In almost every case where the presence of God is promised, it is used as a means of calming and reassuring (Gen 28:15; Deut 31:6–8; 1 Chr 28:20; Matt 28:20; Heb 13:5) When Joshua was taking the command from Moses, God charged him: "Be strong and courageous . . . I am with you." We need to hear that God is with us because we are anxious and fearful people; this leads us to our next section.

Fear

Next, PTSD is composed of a great amount of fear. Fear may seem as a challenge to acknowledge for some and an easy acknowledgement for others. After such gross atrocities that some have experienced, how could fear not be an issue they face? When a person has been continuously traumatized for years, it would seem that fear could easily be a struggle that they face. For those with PTSD, fear often manifests itself in the three-categories of symptoms: avoidance, hyper-arousal, and agitation. Fearful thoughts can lead into avoidance of certain places or activities. Or, fearful thoughts will result in hyper-arousal, which compounds the problem and often makes fear appear to be anger, violence, or irritation when fear is the core of those emotions. Fear is another item that the Bible addresses consistently. In fact, one of the most common imperatives in Scripture is to "fear not" (Luke 12:32).

The Bible—thankfully—does not stop at a "don't" without giving us a "do." That "do" is found in 1 John 4:18: "There is no fear in love, *but perfect love casts out fear*. For fear has to do with punishment, and whoever fears has not been perfected in love [italics mine]." John says they are mutually exclusive. A mature love cannot exist with fear. Without giving a much-needed exposition of this text we can at least determine that the Bible does address the fear that those with PTSD experience.

But even more than love mentioned in 1 John is fear for God. The Scripture tells us that we have an appropriation problem with our fears. Meaning, we appropriate our fears wrongly. Listen to the words of Matthew 10:28, "And do not fear those who kill the body but cannot kill the soul. *Rather fear him* who can destroy both soul and body in hell [italics mine]." We tend to fear wrongly. When we should direct our ultimate fear, honor, and respect towards God alone, we focus that fear on our past circumstances, our memories, certain people, and locations. The inherent problem is not fear. The inherent problem is misappropriated fear. God beckons us to fear him—primarily (Eccl 12:13). So to say this in other words: God commands us to fear and that fear should be directed towards him.

Let this thought offer a shimmer of hope to the ones struggles with fear. God has called them to fear but their fear has been misappropriated. They need to grow in their fear orientation not seek to put their fears to death entirely. Let that be a joy and a challenge. Fear is not the enemy in their struggles; *misappropriated* fear is the enemy. Therefore, "When I am afraid, I put my trust in you" (Ps 56:3). Those suffering from PTSD must learn to re-orient their fear, honor, and reverence to God—not their circumstances, past, or emotions.

INTERPRETING REALITY

One of the last dominant aspects of PTSD is its struggle to interpret reality accurately. Reality often becomes hazy and will only be as clear as the moment allows. The nightmares, the flashbacks, the loud noises, and habituated responses all contribute to this past that seems to live on. The Bible is in the business of helping us interpret reality: that is part of why it exists!

The Bible wants to teach us right thoughts about God and ourselves in response to those thoughts; this is the very essence of interpretation. In fact, Scripture is always superior to our experience or experiences (cf. 2 Pet 1:19). Meaning, those with PTSD must interpret their flashbacks, nightmares, and feelings of vulnerability through the lens of God's Word. Am I in danger? Am I being attacked? Is someone harming me? Will I let Truth guide me or my feelings guide me? Philippians 4:8–9 address how a believer is to think *no matter* what they feel like. As they interpret reality, they must do so through the lens of God's precise description of reality (2 Cor 4:17–18). When those struggling with PTSD are caught in the crossfire of their emotions and truth, they must always subordinate emotions to truth in their interpretation of reality; we walk by faith, not by sight (2 Cor. 5:7). The Bible makes this clear and provides much help in this process.

By now you are probably seeing that the lines of demarcation are not as crisp as we would like them to be when defining PTSD. Ultimately, a myriad of circumstances can lead to a myriad of responses and this is the suffering known as PTSD. In chapter 4 we are going to spend some time unpacking the implications of this statement and how the nature of PTSD is an interpretive disorder. Meaning that you and another person could experience the same traumatic event and only one of you develop PTSD. But to begin that conversation, we should note that we are not to allow this subjectivity to serve as an impetus to minimize or question the reality of the suffering called PTSD. Rather we should cultivate a spirit of grace and understanding. We, as family members, must take a posture like that of God's posture towards us. "The Lord is merciful and gracious, slow to anger and abounding in steadfast love" (Psalm 103:8). We too must be consistent, not sporadic; persistent not disinterested; sensitive not calloused. Although the causes of PTSD are quite subjective and its responses are too, we must never act hastily or crassly towards those with PTSD.

Does the Bible ever use the term post-traumatic stress disorder? No. But it does consistently address fear, anxiety, guilt, and control issues while providing us a framework by which to interpret reality. Perhaps you think at this point that I am being a little simplistic in my approach or, the Bible's approach to PTSD. That is always a consideration of wise biblical help, yet we must not confuse simplicity with being simplistic. The Bible cogently addresses the problems of man and once we cut our way through the muddy terminology that often clouds man's problems, we can see clearly and apply the Bible accurately. This is not being overly simplistic but rather being clear and simple. Let us not muddy the waters of PTSD in an effort to seem intellectually savvy or original. Rather, let us take what the Bible says about man to be true and accurate and then apply that to the problems of PTSD—to the glory of God!

Chapter 3

A History of PTSD

It's important to recognize that PTSD is not a new phenomenon. In this chapter we will attempt to show some of the history of both trauma and PTSD. My goal is to set this conversation in context of historical perspective. The biggest takeaway from this chapter is for you to understand that what your loved one is facing is, in fact, "common to man" (1 Cor 10:13). God has been faithful to others who have faced severe suffering and he will be faithful to them, as well. To begin, let's take a look at trauma and some of the ways trauma has been viewed.

A HISTORY OF TRAUMA

Like PTSD, trauma is definitely not a new phenomenon to mankind. Dr. Allan Young, professor of Social Studies in Medicine, says that

> A new kind of memory was born, at the intersection of two streams of scientific inquiry: somatic and psychological. The somatic stream dates from the 1860s and the discovery of a previously unidentified kind of assault, called "nervous shock." The psychological stream begins earlier, in the 1790s, and leads to the discovery of a previously unidentified kind of forgetting, called 'repression'

and 'dissociation.' By the 1890s, nervous shock and re-
pression/dissociation have been conjoined to produce
the traumatic memory. . . . [1]

Dr. Young is suggesting that in the eighteenth century traumatic memory finds its roots, but at a very rudimentary level, traumatic memory is an age-old discussion. Genocide, abuse, racial
conflicts, holy wars, jihadists, and despots have all contributed to
the trauma that so many have endured in their lifetime. Trauma is
the hinge on which PTSD rotates, on that most doctors and scholars would agree but what is trauma?

Trauma is defined as:

> Direct personal experience of an event that involves ac-
> tual or threatened death or serious injury, or other threat
> to one's physical integrity; or witnessing an event that
> involves death, injury, or a threat to the physical integ-
> rity of another person; or learning about unexpected or
> violent death, serious harm, or threat of death or injury
> experienced by a family member or other close associate
> (Criterion A1). The person's response to the event must
> involve intense fear, helplessness, or horror (or in chil-
> dren, the response must involve disorganized or agitated
> behavior). . . . [2]

Or, in simpler terms, "a deeply disturbing or distressing
experience."[3] Trauma at its very core is an extremely distressing
circumstance that a person intimately experiences. Whether it
happened to them or someone they know, trauma has a serious
amount of pain associated with its definition and is not limited to
one event or a history of events.

1. Young, *Harmony of Illusions*, 13.

2. Sage Publications, "What is Trauma?"

3. Apple Dictionary 2.2.1, s.v. "trauma." Also see the APA's definition of
trauma as, "Trauma is an emotional response to a terrible event like an accident, rape or natural disaster." American Psychological Association, "Trauma."

TRAUMA AS AN EVENT OR LIFESTYLE

Westerner's think of trauma in terms of an event, whereas those in third-world countries often think of trauma as a way of life. Car bombs, vigilantes, land mines, and gangs do not come and go—they only come. Dr. Nancy Styvendale has argued that trauma cannot always be associated to a singular, recognizable, and chronologically bound incident. This thought revolutionizes some of the modern conceptions of trauma or a *trigger event* that lead to PTSD. The family ministering must be cognizant that for some, trauma is so ingrained in their way of life that to isolate one trigger event would be functionally impossible.[4] An example of this can be taken from the Cambodians who suffered under the Khmer Rouge.

The Reign of Terror

From 1975 to 1979 the Khmer Rouge inflicted some of the worst atrocities known to modern history on their own people. Mass executions, rapes, murders, starvation, famine, and a socialistic society were all offshoots of what the Khmer Rouge inflicted on its people. For years the Cambodian people have lived with the effects of the Khmer Rouge and the trauma they inflicted, sometimes reminded by an uncovered landmine that was originally planted years ago.

Dr. Grant Marshall led an investigation that surveyed the largest group of Cambodian people living in America. In the survey he found that out of 490 people age 35–75, "99 percent nearly starved to death, 96 percent were place in forced labor, which was equal to enslavement, 90 percent had a family member or friend murdered, and 54 percent were tortured. Even after arriving in the U.S., 34 percent said they had seen a dead body in their neighborhood."[5] The Cambodians that survived the reign of terror from the Khmer Rouge can undoubtedly show that trauma is not only an event, it is a way of life.

---

4. However, this book will provide a template of sorts in addressing perpetual suffering in Chapter 7.

5. The National Institute of Mental Health, "PTSD and Depression Epidemic Among Cambodian Immigrants."

Homelessness

Another author has suggested that trauma can, in fact, be a persistent way of life. Take the homeless for instance. Dr. Josephine Martin has stated that, "Homelessness—not having a home, a place to live—shatters the basic security all humans require for adequate personality development and good mental health. Loss of a home, particularly as a result of fire, constitutes a psychic trauma that frequently results in an acute or chronic stress disorder." This too helps revolutionize the thought that trauma is an event; her claims are that trauma is a lifestyle for some. In a very real sense, this opens the floodgates for traumatic events to take any form or shape.

Poverty

Poverty has too been seen as a traumatic event. Arne Eide took a survey of the level of pain associated with both with Cambodian land mine survivors who were not subject to poverty and those who lived in abject poverty after exposure to a land mine. He noted that "We can stop bleeding and heal wounds, and should, of course, do our best to heal more wounds. *But poverty acts as a trauma beyond our control* [italics mine]."[6] The trauma of poverty has served to make the trauma of exposure to landmines worse as hospital bills, inability to work, and handicapped families struggle to make ends meet.

Eide further states that, "In traditional Euro-representations, the massacres, fire bombings of civilians, and silent killings by mines represent the extraordinary but for the victims, those incidents are ordinary—death is normal."[7] He draws out how the typical Western mindset holds to trauma as an event whereas the victims of such atrocities often view the trauma as a way of life, as normal.

---

6. Eide, *Disability and Poverty*, 213.

7. Ibid., 215.

Conclusion

Traumatic events are both events and life-styles as we have seen above. Some people experience trauma at the event level, while others experience trauma at the lifestyle level; what is important is that trauma must not be seen only as an isolated incident. Trauma is a very real part of human experience and it cannot be forced into a specific context at specific times—the lines of trauma get extremely blurred for some people. Ask the North Korean in the gulag, ask the Syrian refugee, or ask the child of an abusive parent and you will see that trauma never left, it only came. The wise family member must be sensitive to the life of suffering that their loved one may have experienced while seeking to help them to biblically make sense of it all.

The History of PTSD

PTSD is not a new phenomenon or experience, only the term PTSD is new. In the Civil War "nostalgia" and "soldier's heart" were the titles that described the PTSD-like symptoms. In World War I "the effort syndrome" and "chronic fatigue syndrome" summarized what some soldiers in combat were facing. In addition to the "effort syndrome" and "chronic fatigue syndrome" in WWI, "shellshock" became a more popular term to summarize the mental and physical wounds of those involved in combat with "Post-Vietnam Syndrome" being the way PTSD was articulated in the late sixties to early seventies. "Post Traumatic Stress Disorder" finally became the diagnosis coined in 1980 under the American Psychiatric Association's *Diagnostic and Statistical Manual of Mental Disorders III*.

Dr. Mathew Freidmen from The Department of Veteran's Affairs gives a brief history of PTSD by stating that:

> The risk of exposure to trauma has been a part of the human condition since we evolved as a species. Attacks by saber tooth tigers or twenty-first century terrorists have probably produced similar psychological sequelae in the survivors of such violence. Shakespeare's Henry IV

appears to meet many, if not all, of the diagnostic criteria for Post-traumatic Stress Disorder (PTSD), as have other heroes and heroines throughout the world's literature.

In 1980, the American Psychiatric Association (APA) added PTSD to the third edition of its Diagnostic and Statistical Manual of Mental Disorders (DSM-III) nosologic classification scheme. Although controversial when first introduced, the PTSD diagnosis has filled an important gap in psychiatric theory and practice. From an historical perspective, the significant change ushered in by the PTSD concept was the stipulation that the etiological agent was outside the individual (i.e., a traumatic event) rather than an inherent individual weakness (i.e., a traumatic neurosis).[8]

PTSD, as Dr. Freidmen has observed, is a struggle that mankind has faced from its early years. While we might disagree with some of his evolutionary thinking or his originations of PTSD, we can easily observe that PTSD is no new phenomenon but only its prevalence and vernacular are new phenomenon.

It is also noteworthy that PTSD has been so deeply rooted in a military or combat related context that there exists a potential to separate the symptoms of non-military individuals. Yet, this must not be so if the APA's definition of PTSD is to be accepted. While military personnel are prone to such symptoms, victims of car accidents, abuse, natural disaster survivors, and any other form of life-threatening trauma are still candidates for PTSD. The association of PTSD and the military will grow increasingly distant as the prevalence of PTSD continues to grow. Meaning, PTSD is bigger than combat. Ultimately trauma and PTSD are not new experiences of man, just the vernacular is new. This encourages us to see that God has been faithful to others who have faced difficult experiences, and he'll do the same for our loved ones.

8. Friedmen, "PTSD History and Overview."

Chapter 4

Helping Our Family Member Interpret Reality

PTSD AS AN INTERPRETIVE PHENOMENON

HAVE YOU EVER WONDERED why two different individuals can experience the same circumstance and one develops PTSD and the other does not? Secular psychologists point to a plethora of suggestions on why this may be so, beginning with genetics and moving to sociological and cultural influences. Meaning, different cultures respond to trauma in different ways and there is a possibility that a culture can worsen the symptoms of PTSD rather than help those with PTSD. Yet, does that answer the proposed question?

What I suggest is that *PTSD is an interpretive disorder*, meaning that the way one *perceives* the threat determines their response to the threat. To say it another way, the interpretation of the circumstances determines the response to the circumstances.

I grew up in Savannah, Georgia and had the privilege of serving as a pastor there in recent years. In Savannah, I had fellow Army friends that were part of the Special Operations community within the military. What I learned in my time and ministry with them is that the Special Operations guys wanted to be in traumatic experiences—combat. Granted, I was a communications officer when I was in the Army and I wanted to be in garrison so this is hard for me to understand! However, these guys looked forward to going to the fight and were saddened when they couldn't. Not only saddened, but almost shameful. They saw honor, they saw duty, and they had an inner obligation to be with their unit in the middle of traumatic environments. These guys looked forward to being part of traumatic experiences, and illustrated that PTSD is an interpretive disorder. What most would see as traumatizing they were eager to be a part of. They faced all kinds of traumatic experiences, yet the majority of them wanted to be a part of these experiences and experienced greater turmoil when they were forced to stay behind. It was more traumatizing to stay home, than it was to go to combat for these guys.

This is true in the medical profession, as well. Think of the carnage that medical doctors regularly see in the operating room. Why is that not traumatizing for them? It's not traumatizing because of how they interpret it. One medical doctor, Dr. Charles Hodges, said that:

> I recently talked with an individual who compared two events in life. Both were bad and resulted in death. One event was a PTSD source and the other was not. The difference was that one victim was young and the other was . . . very old. The young man did not have the opportunity to live that the old man did. So the older man's death did not affect the individual the same way the death of the young man. So, in that sense it is interpretive.
>
> As a physician, I have witnessed amazingly terrible events, like open-heart surgery; it doesn't bother me. In another context seeing someone's chest torn open might bother a great deal. So, *that interpretation depends on context* [italics mine].[1]

Dr. Hodges affirms that the way we view our circumstance encourages the effect the circumstance has on an individual. In the middle

1. Hodges, Personal Correspondence, May 16, 2013.

of a traumatic event, people are seeking to make sense out of the terrible things they are experiencing; they are meaning-makers. So the way they make that meaning is by interpreting their circumstances. This interpretive work is at the center of the problem and solution of PTSD. Yet what other factors may be contributing to these conclusions?

INFLUENCES OF INTERPRETATION

Genetic Predisposition

Scholars also believe that genetic composition leads to a predisposition towards PTSD. Dr. Armen Goenjian, a research professor of psychiatry at the Semel Institute for Neuroscience and Human Behavior at UCLA, observed the following comments:

> [He] analyzed DNA from 200 adults from Armenia who survived the devastating 1988 earthquake. The people spanned several generations and were from twelve extended families who suffered PTSD symptoms after the disaster. The families' genes showed that those who had specific variants of two genes were more prone to PTSD symptoms. The genes, called TPH1 and TPH2, control the production of serotonin. Serotonin is a brain chemical that regulates mood, sleep and alertness; all of these are disrupted in PTSD.[2]

His suggestion is that genetic composition and those who have specific variants of certain genes are predisposed to PTSD. This adds layers of complexities and drives a need for further research but what must be observed is that there are—potentially genetic—reasons that certain people interpret events one way and reasons another person interprets an event differently. Although, I do not agree with these findings in their entirety, I do agree that physiological influences could encourage a certain interpretation of events. In addition, another consideration is social influences.

---

2. Shepherd, "Post-traumatic Stress Disorder Linked to Genetics."

Social Influences

Social influences are another shaping factor into how we interpret trauma. Culture teaches people how to be interpreters, whether a person realizes it or not. It conveys meaning and provides paradigms (think of the culture of the Special Operations community mentioned above). Culture often tells us what a traumatic event even looks like and, in some cultures, it tells us how we should respond to those traumatic events. Dr. Robert Muller of York University noted that:

> Immediately following the tsunami [referring to the 2004 tsunami], Sri Lankan peoples' top priority seemed to be aiding those around them, rather than seeking treatment themselves, behaviors that were viewed by many of the therapists as signs of "denial" and "shock," and considered to be warning signs of PTSD. Despite the persistence of Sri Lankans to continue helping those around them, the therapists continued encouraging them to stop and "take care of themselves first." However, in many cultures, the practice is to help others before you help yourself.[3]

The culture of the Sri Lankans encouraged how they responded to the trauma of such a horrific natural disaster. Consequently, the culture shaped how the Sri Lankans interpreted the tsunami and, as Dr. Muller noted, prevented the development of what he would call a 'psychological' problem.

Can it be that culture contributes significantly to PTSD? Anthony Marsella of the University of Hawaii says that a "reasonable point of view is that all disorders are culture-bound, including all Western disorders since they emerge, are experienced, and responded to within a cultural context. The question must be asked: Can any psychological disorder escape cultural influence? The answer is: No!"[4] Some have said that Western attempt to transpose PTSD and its symptoms on other cultures is creating a "tyranny"

---

3. Muller, "Culture & PTSD: Lessons from the 2004 Tsunami."
4. Marsella, "Ethnocultural Aspects of PTSD," 17–24.

of sorts that ultimately hurts the local culture.[5] A biblical response is that yes, society and culture do influence the interpretation of trauma and that influence may not always be a positive one, but it's never a determinative one.[6]

Other Influences

Familial influences are another significant factor to how a person responds to PTSD, or how they interpret trauma that, in turn, determines if they develop PTSD. This influence can range from the frequency of trauma experienced in a family to the way the family ministers to one who has been exposed to traumatic events. Do they minimize the circumstance? Do they exacerbate the pain? Do they help the family member respond to the circumstances or do they seek to avoid the circumstances like the plague? These are all factors that shape the influence of interpretation of traumatic events, and are important considerations in your ministry to family members.

Frequency of exposure to traumatic events is inevitably a factor in the interpretation of those events. Are they normative? As mentioned above, is it a lifestyle of trauma or an isolated incident of PTSD? In conducting an informal survey, I found that divorce is quite traumatic for young children whose parents are separating for the first time. Yet, two divorces later there is not as much negative associations with the divorce. Why? The reason is because of the *frequency of exposure* to traumatic events. In both instances your parents are separating from their spouse, consequent moves transpire, separation from family occurs, and emotional pain follows. Yet, both instances do not carry the same weight of trauma—there is a difference in interpretation due to frequent exposure, or pre-existing exposure.

5. Ibid., 18.

6. However, a biblical response does not believe that society and culture are determinative, or with the definitions of these cited researchers. Both use PTSD in terms of a deterministic "psychological" disorder, which tugs at the very way the Scripture would describe man and his problems.

Religious Influences

One of the most intriguing observations from secular scholars is that religious influences are some of the greater influences in how we interpret trauma and respond to trauma. Dr. Chen, assistant professor at West Point military academy, notes that, "Four of the eleven studies reviewed [the majority] reported positive associations between measures of religion/spirituality and PTSD—higher scores on one measure were correlated with higher scores on the other."[7] Note these were not tests conducted by him but rather his observations from an assortment of eleven different surveys. Yet, he does note that the majority of the research proves that a person's religiosity affects their interpretation of trauma and, consequently, PTSD.

Two professors, one from University of California Berkley and the other from University of California San Francisco, observe very similar happenings. They say that:

> The two most influential cognitively oriented formulations of trauma response and recovery highlight either the *importance of beliefs and linked emotions about the self and the world* . . . or the network of associations linking thinking about or reminders of a traumatic event to cognitive, emotional, physiological, and behavioral responses . . . [italics mine].[8]

The "beliefs and linked emotions" are the worldview through which a person interprets life—and in our discussion—trauma. Beliefs about the world and self are none other than a religious conviction, whether one sees God as the primary actor or not. Religion is a way of viewing the world and self; consequently, people are inherently religious (Rom 1).

Romans 1 states that all people are worshippers. In Romans 1:23 we see that the problem is not a lack of religion, it is the wrong manifestation of that religion. The orientation of that religion is what is so egregious and indicative of the Lord turning them over

7. Chen, "Traumatic Stress and Religion," 375–76.

8. Ozer and Weiss, "Who Develops Posttraumatic Stress Disorder?," 169.

to their own desires (1:18). All people view life concerning themselves and the world through a religious paradigm; the question is who is their god not do they worship a god.

We can conclude there is an importance of religious beliefs in the way that a person synthesizes the events of their life. It's my goal to press upon you, as the reader, that in order for families to support each other through the trials of PTSD, they must have right beliefs about self, the world, and God. Without these essential parts of your family's ministry, your efforts may show temporary fruit but will hold no lasting value. You will be momentarily pleased with what seems like great progress only to see the façade of 'healing' come crashing down on your family. The way that you minister best to your loved one experiencing PTSD is not to avoid talks of religion, but as seen above, to engage them through proper religion.

In conclusion, there are many shaping influences into how a person interprets trauma, which in turn determines the development of PTSD. There is much research to be done to articulate whether or not there are genetic predispositions, what the culture teaches, and how families contribute towards or detract from PTSD. It is important that the Christian family doesn't accept the so-called findings of the secular researchers without discretion and caution remembering all these influences are still just influences. Perhaps there is truth to their findings, yet their findings do not function as the authority. Only Scripture can do that. Can circumstances, family, or culture cause PTSD? No, it can't; it can only encourage it.

Therefore, what we can note are the following: (1) PTSD necessitates trauma, (2) trauma demands interpretation, and (3) interpretation determines PTSD. It is one's own personal interpretation of the traumatic event that determines whether or not they feel their life to be threatened or are in a position of great vulnerability. PTSD is an interpretive phenomenon, even if there are genetic or cultural predispositions involved.

Chapter 5

Peering through the Fog of Interpretation

As I went to work in the early morning there was nothing spectacular about it. The alarm clock barged into my sleep and I grabbed my uniform and slung my rucksack over my shoulder. We had a ruck march that morning and were commemorating the 60th anniversary of the start of the Korean War. As we walked that morning it was uniquely strange. We wove through the Korean mountains on our ruck march and I could not help but be enamored by the thick fog that surrounded us. We thought how unsuspecting the South would have been that Sunday morning so many years before. We saw how the thick Korean fog shrouded so much: mountains, paths, trails, and roads. It was unique in that we saw the fog and did not see because of the fog.

One of the unique factors of PTSD is that because of its interpretive nature, we have to enter into the fog of our family member's interpretation with biblical wisdom. At times the fog is thicker than others, or thicker for certain loved ones. They see the fog and do not see because of the fog. However, they do see—barely. Like the sun burning off the early morning fog that day on our ruck march, we must come with biblical wisdom that assimilates what happened to them and how they can respond to those circumstances. We also inform families on how they can best serve their loved one, perhaps you are that family and this work is providing that information to you. Yet, the loved one must also see that that their family member does not see, at least not entirely or clearly.

TRUTH VS. FEELINGS

The family of the one with PTSD has to orient their loved one around truth. Truth enters into the world of emotions and organizes the thoughts. "What if I had done this? I should have just done that. If only they would not of. . . . " Regret, guilt, rehashing the circumstance, and reliving the trauma are part of what makes PTSD so painful. The mental torture, for some, is worse than the actual trauma. Consequently, the family member must communicate grace and truth to them; truth that orients and guides; truth that also assimilates and organizes their trauma. We will discuss how to interact with guilt, regret, rehashing, reliving, and some of the other intensely emotional experiences. But first we must start with the premise that truth is the beacon of light shining through the fog of interpretation. Even when we do not know what lies around the next turn, we can still see the direction of the light.

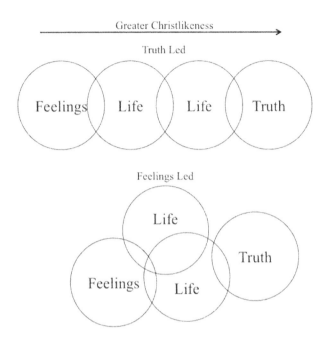

Figure 1. Truth vs. Feelings Led

Truth must always be the guide in both our lives and the lives of our family members. One way that I like to describe that process is using the links of a chain (cf. Figure 1). If you pull the first link in a chain, the remaining links will follow. Yet, if you push the last link in an effort to move the chain forward everything gets out of alignment. In the same way, our family members must know that when truth leads their life—not feelings—they will be moving the direction God wants them to move, which is toward greater Christlikeness (2 Cor 5:7). But if they try to push forward with their feelings, life gets pretty messy. The bottom line is that truth must guide feelings, or to say it another way: truth must interpret and direct feelings. Yes, your feelings may not line up with truth but they will—eventually. And even if your feelings never align, do not succumb to the temptation to invert this process and let your feelings steer your life. We are called to walk by faith, not feelings.

In this process we are calling our family member to a new paradigm of thinking: truth thinking. Not only is the Word of God true (Ps 19:9b) but also that the Word of God is the measure of what is truth (John 17:17). The Word of God sets the standard for truth and then meets that standard. This is the robust capability of the Scriptures to define and then to fulfill. Consequently, we bring our family members to this model of truth so that they can see things as God sees them and respond to them as God would have them respond to them.

One of the most helpful methods of doing this is by employing some type of way by which we are to "take thoughts captive" (2 Cor 10:5). In Second Corinthians 10:5 Paul speaks of his ministry in taking thoughts captive to obey Christ. The idea is that he is forcefully taking thoughts in captivity to the lordship of Christ: forcing those that would rise up against the knowledge of God into obedience. I often describe for people that we can imagine this by thinking of a fence into which we are forcing our thoughts to become obedient to Christ. Fencing your thoughts in with God's truth is the idea. Literally, forcing them to be within the confines of God's truth. We are to take our thoughts and fence them in with the truth of God. Philippians 4:8 gives us the slats of that fence in saying, "Finally, brothers, whatever is true, whatever is honorable, whatever is just, whatever is pure, whatever is lovely, whatever is commendable, if there is any excellence, if there is anything worthy of praise, think about these things." Paul has given a clear and systematic approach to a wandering thought life and Figure 2 represents an illustration that could easily be used for a family member suffering from PTSD.

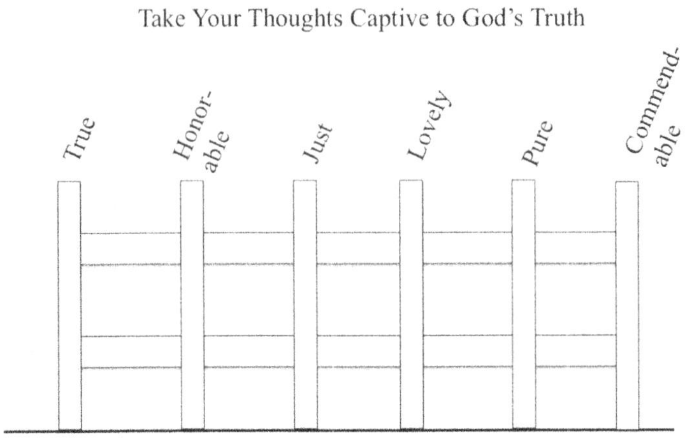

Take Your Thoughts Captive to God's Truth

Figure 2. Fencing Your Truth in with God's Truth

In taking our thoughts captive, we must force them into submission to Christ with the help of the Holy Spirit. When we believe something that is not true, it escapes from the bounds of this fence. When we allow untruthful thoughts to dominate our thinking, we are not taking our thoughts captive to God's truth. Thus, we force our thoughts into captivity by asking, "Is this true? Is this just? Is what I am thinking honorable?" When those thoughts are not corresponding to Philippians 4:8, we must force them into captivity of God's truth. God's truth must prevail upon what we believe; God's truth must prevail upon our truth!

The one suffering with PTSD must begin to employ some sort of method that encourages them to address their thought life and reorient it to God's truth. Essentially we are saying that we believe what God says about our circumstances, then by faith we are seeking to be obedient to what he is called us to do. That is taking our thoughts captive to Christ. Let's take John for example.

A CASE STUDY: JOHN AND PTSD

John served in the infantry in the thick of Iraq, 2008.[1] He was excited to go and put into practice his training. There was no morbid desire to exact vengeance, just an excitement to be an infantryman. Yet after four months in the Middle East, the excitement slowly faded. What he saw was not as bad as the regret he experienced. While he was serving in Iraq he experienced egregious things. Things that expose the nastiness of combat and the havoc it wreaks on a person. Those were bad. Yet, what bothered him was not the carnage of battle but the war crimes he saw his superiors sanction while they were in Iraq. He saw women molested by NATO forces, civilians abused, and a myriad of other crimes during his tour. Now he lives with the thoughts of regret for not blowing the whistle while he served in the military. It is has been eight years since he was in Iraq and three since he was honorably discharged from the Army. Now he is distanced with his kids, Mark and Shelby, and easily agitated with Veronica, his wife. John struggles to sleep on some nights and still experiences what has been termed *hyper-arousal*. Just the other day his son slammed the front door and John instantly went back to the height of the war in 2005 and saw those horrific scenes on the replay reel of his mind.

So how do we help John? First, we would instill biblical hope (something we will spend a lot of time on in Chapter 6). John is not someone who could be characterized by flagrant rebellion but weakness (1 Thess 5:14). He is not actively choosing to torment himself, yet, at some level he is choosing to revisit these dark corners of his life. We should show him that he is not the only one to experience the egregious things of life and take him to some of the biblical examples mentioned above (e.g., Paul, David, and Joseph).

Next, we would get right at his struggles. What happened . . . in detail? There are a few very real possibilities: (1) John did participate in sinful activities while he was serving in Iraq, (2) he was acting as a minister of the Lord to punish evildoers at a global

---

1. John's story is a combination of multiple stories to protect identity and provide illustration.

level (Rom 13:1–7), or (3) some combination of the two aspects where John did act wrongly on certain occasions but on other occasions did what he should have done. John needs help in sorting out reality or even reinterpreting reality according to God's truth (i.e., fencing his thoughts in with God's truth). It is important to draw out what our family member has experienced so that you can proceed with understanding and insight. This applies for all forms of trauma—rape, natural disaster, abuse, and so forth. We have to know as much as is necessary to understand our family member's traumatic experience; this may be a slow process depending on the circumstance, but it is still a direct process meaning that is where we must go and we must get there quickly.

In John's case, I found that he did allow innocent people to be harmed without intervening or contacting the appropriate authorities. So, we walked through repentance and confession starting in Psalm 32:5 and 1 John 1:9. The guiding principle was that his confession needed to be as public as his sin. In this case, at least two-dozen men were aware of this sin—most of whom he did not know how to get in touch with if he wanted. This was not going to be easy.

So we worked together to write a legal statement and turn it into the Judge Advocate General (JAG). As we did this, we were going to trust that God would work as far as he would want this investigation to proceed. John could not start an investigation; that was responsibility of the JAG office. The only thing he could do was state what he observed in this incident. While he may never see the families that were wronged by his comrades, he would offer restitution through this act of transparency and repentance. This gave him hope as he previously debated on flying back to Iraq just to formally seek the forgiveness of those families. The principle that I followed here was to seek to offer restitution for the wrongs he committed as best as he could.[2] While it would make his life a little more difficult, potentially, he was not in the wrong with the law but did sin in that he did not stop the incident or report the incident to the authorities.

---

2. Cf. Sande's *The Peacemaker* in Appendix C for some good principles on biblical restitution.

After starting the principles of restitution John needed a lot of help in taming his wild thoughts. We implemented the idea of taking his thoughts captive to God's truth, as provided above, and started building the *think and do* list. This list simply has three columns with a put off, be renewed, and put on column. We started to have him list the thoughts with which he struggles, what God would have him think (e.g., a Scripture), and how he should respond. It was helpful for John to hear more than, "Don't think that way." He needed some real, practical ways of responding to the thoughts that plague his life.

SOFTENING THE SEEMINGLY DEFINITIVE

What was part of John's struggle is the spinning-of-the-wheels thought pattern coupled with the fact that the Army psychologists told him he had PTSD—the end. There was no cure, there was no remedy; there was only a diagnosis that now has become the determiner. What a person struggling with PTSD needs to hear is that there is hope for change, lasting and authentic change. There is hope for a life that is identified not by their traumatic circumstances but by what happened on behalf of them through a traumatic circumstance—the cross.

The question they must ask themselves is: "Will this circumstance define who I am or will my identity in Christ define who I am?" This must be answered upfront. When a person believes that their identity is not in their diagnosis, but rather as a creature, in Christ, who has been justified, adopted, made a new creation, currently a saint who is a servant of God, and is not yet perfect, they will realize there is hope for change. To put it succinctly, as a believer they are in Christ and are consequently a new creation. This is their banner and identity, not their disorder.

When our family member begins to reorient the interpretation of their identity, they will subtly soften the seemingly definitive. No longer will it be an "I have a disorder" mentality but "I have a weakness."[3] Through the grace of God, the event that has

3. Welch, *Blame it on the Brain*, 53–56.

shaped their life will become an event that leads them to greater Christlikeness. They will see that they are not determined by what happened to them in their trauma but by what happened to them in their union with Christ. Consequently, a white-knuckled grasp of their diagnosis must not be clung to as they seek to sort through the interpretation of what happened. There must be a softening of the seemingly definitive as they understand the applicable biblical truth.

This whole process of reinterpreting the traumatic event falls within the framework of contextualizing suffering as mentioned in Chapter 1. We are not seeking to avoid suffering, ignore suffering, or minimize suffering. Rather, we are seeking to *contextualize* suffering. The trauma that some have faced is bone-chillingly evil. We must sympathize with their suffering. We have to pause and weep over the pain they endured—sometimes repeatedly. Yet,

> Here again we follow the example of Christ's love for us. The grace that adopts me into Christ's family is not a grace that says I am okay. In fact, the Bible is clear that God extends his grace to me because I am everything but okay. . . . We sturdily refuse to condemn, but we also refuse to condone. We accept people [and contextualize their suffering] with a grace that empowers us for God's work of heart change.[4]

Our effort to reorient their interpretation and contextualize their suffering is one that has an agenda. That agenda is to help them see the way God is working in their life to make them more like Christ.

In the next few chapters we will spend more time in the *how* of that agenda but suffice it for now to say that there is an interpretation that will need to be reoriented. We must peer through the fog of interpretation, which implies we will have to interact the actual trauma as best as possible. Yet, this effort is one that seeks to lovingly understand and graciously contextualize. We are to teach them they are shaped by the trauma they have experienced but not determined by it. In this truth, the counselee should find much hope, which is exactly where our studies take us next.

4. Tripp, *Instrument's in the Redeemer's Hands*, 158–59.

Chapter 6

Instilling Hope

"A bruised reed he will not break,

and a faintly burning wick he will not quench;

he will faithfully bring forth justice."

—ISAIAH 42:3

THE BRUISED REED

MANY SUFFERING WITH PTSD are bruised reeds. They can feel the weight of their sufferings and at times, it pummels them to the ground as the try to endure. A reed was a plant very similar to what the modern reader would associate with bamboo. In its biblical usage, it represented shifty, weak, and unstable people (Isa 42:3; Matt 12:20). Isaiah prophesied that the Lord will not break off the weak person who with every gust of wind—or life—almost falls but rather he will beckon them to come to Himself for rest (Matt 11:28–30). Those suffering with PTSD need something that no secular science or prescription medication can give them; they need hope, lasting biblical hope.

Hope has become somewhat passé in its biblical employment. Substituted is a whimsical anticipation that something good will transpire out of life's events. "I hope you have a good day at work" your wife tells you as you leave the house. "Don't get your hopes up" the teacher tells his ambitious students. What about the sufferer of PTSD? How does hope apply to their seemingly hopeless situation? If we are to give any help to those suffering with PTSD, we must recognize that true, biblical hope is an integral part of the Christian faith, which sets God as its object and the promises he has made its foundation. The sufferer of PTSD needs to know that their hope is directed to a good God who does what he says, especially in the times of suffering that they may experience.

WHAT IS BIBLICAL HOPE?

When we think of hope there is often an idea of "desired outcome (akin to 'wishful thinking')"[1] as mentioned previously (cf. 3 John 14). "I hope things get better" or perhaps, "I hope you enjoy the vacation!" These are both common phrases that one would expect to hear in a modern context of the word *hope*. However, when the Bible approaches hope, it does it with a few aspects in mind that often are expressed in other English words like, "wait, trust, expectation and confidence." In fact, for the English speaker these are almost separate in totality from what we would consider hope to be, or for some these words are simply subcategories of hope. What is a biblical definition of hope? To be sure, one must start with the Old Testament and then progress into the New Testament teachings of hope to understand how the majority of believers would have understood hope.

In the Old Testament, hope is used in multiple ways. Ways that vary often in our English equivalent to the word hope. In some cases it has the idea of a waiting, as seen in Job 13:15, "Though he slay me, I will hope in him." Other times the word hope conjures up the idea of God being the "hope of Israel" (Jer 14:8, 17:3) with

---

1. Freedman, Myers and Beck, *Eerdmans Dictionary of the Bible*, s.v. "hope."

all of its end-time implications. Hope in these Jeremiah passages refers explicitly to God being that Hope.[2] He is the confidence of Israel, the "expectation."[3] While other times God himself promises that he will give hope (Jer 29:11). At one point, Job claims that "he has pulled up my hope like a tree" (Job 19:10), referring to God uprooting hope in this passage. Lastly, the idea of help for someone is also a way in which hope is employed (Prov 26:12). So as we read the Old Testament, there is a multi-faceted employment of the English word "hope" but Walther Zimmerli summarizes it well by saying that, "According to the Old Testament faith, hope is only legitimate where God remains the sole Lord, in activity, in gift and in promise, and where man anticipates the future in no other way than as the free gift of God."[4]

In the New Testament, hope is used in very similar contexts as the Old Testament but with more clarification as to whom and in what hope is based. Hope is seen as essential (1 Pet 1:3–9), as an anchor (Heb 6:19), and as one of the main elements of Christian character (1 Cor 13:13; faith, hope, and love). Perhaps this adds clarity to the fact that faith and love are said to originate in hope (Col 1:4–5) and also that all who do not believe in Christ have no hope (Eph 2:12; 1 Thess 4:13). Summarily, it can be said that New Testament hope is an essential characteristic of the Christian faith whose object is Christ and whose fulfillment will be at the return of Christ, as promised in Scripture.

Hope is an all-encompassing term that the Bible uses to articulate an expectation in who God is and how he fulfills his promises. Dr. Stuart Scott provides one of the best definitions of the nature of biblical hope. In a sermon entitled "Biblical Hope in Discouragement" he states that hope is "An effectual confidence in who God is and an eager anticipation of God's promise to bring us to himself, even in the face of very difficult circumstances."[5] Our

---

2. Also see Psalm 62:5 for similar terminology.

3. Gesenius and Tregelles, *Gesenius' Hebrew and Chaldee Lexicon to the Old Testament Scriptures*.

4. Zimmerli, *Man and His Hope in the Old Testament*, 24.

5. Scott, "Biblical Hope in Discouragement Part 1."

family member suffering with PTSD must know that the reason they can have hope is not because of their experiences, their doctors, or their own inner determinedness. Their hope is based off of the character of God and his promises.

OUR HOPE IS BUILT ON NOTHING LESS

The differences between biblical hope and the hope of this world are vast. Biblical hope is built on the character of God and his promises, while worldly hope is built on circumstances, medications, 'coping better', and doctors. The focus of worldly hope is inherently temporal whereas the orientation of biblical hope is inherently Godward focused. Worldly hope is consistently a whimsical aspiration, "if it only were true" mentality, while mixed with concrete expectations placed in wrong objects. Biblical hope is a concrete expectation (1 Thess 4:13) in proper objects, namely, God and his promises. Although the hope of the world may be future oriented, others oriented, or positively oriented, it will not be oriented on the grounds of God's character and the work and return of Jesus Christ.

Worldly hope or hope of this world is not based off of the work of Jesus Christ (1 Pet 1:3), the resurrection of Christ (1 Pet 3:21; 1 Cor 15:17), and most certainly the hope of this world is not based on the return of Christ (1 Pet 1:13; Tit. 2:13). So while the object of worldly hope is different, even the means of worldly hope is inherently different. Scripture often refers to hope as being formed in the furnace of adversity (Rom 5:3–4), kindled by the Scriptures (Rom 15:4), and applied by the Holy Spirit (Rom 15:13).

Why does all of this matter? You will be of no help to your loved one if you only offer them circumstantial, whimsical, flimsy hope. Their hope is built on nothing less than the character of God and his promises. We cannot truly be helpful in our ministry to them by helping them orient their hope around medications, or new doctors. Their hope is not that they can learn to cope. Their hope is built off of the faithfulness of God and his promise that he will give grace in our trials (1 Cor 10:13).

REGAINING HOPE FOR THE HOPELESS

When hope has been lost what should we do? When approaching this question one must not be presumptuous as if there were an antidote for hopelessness that could be taken and "poof," hope has been restored. It is in the daily despair—the PTSD flashback of that terrible day—that the answer to this question is concerned, in the dark moments of life. It is not a solution one can ungraciously smack on their hopelessness but is a process of reorienting the wayward ship towards God, lest it be dashed on the rocks of despair.

Often it is the thinking of the hopeless that contributes to the perpetual hopelessness they are experiencing. It may be true that the hopeless do not *want* to change their thinking. They believe they are the victims, they have rights and their circumstances are not fair. At some level, this may be an accurate assessment; they may be in unfair circumstances that victimize them. They have been wronged and sometimes egregiously so. Ultimately, however, they have gone astray in proper thinking by choosing to dwell on those facts in a way that is unbiblical and ultimately dishonoring to God. The hopeless need to reorient their thinking to truth as mentioned above.

In the restoration of hope there must be a correction of thinking that either confirms a biblical understanding of hope exists, institutes a biblical understanding of hope, or both. This does not imply that every person who has lost hope does not understand hope but merely that one must first confirm that hope is properly understood before proceeding to implementation.

A good illustration of restoring hope is seen in Luke 24. The disciples "hoped" (Luke 24:21) that this Jesus was their Redeemer but lost that hope because his crucifixion, despite the accounts of his tomb being empty. Jesus came along side of them and oriented them back to the Scriptures. Scripture says, "And their eyes were opened, and they recognized him" (Luke 24:31). Christ provided hope by "beginning with Moses and all the Prophets, he interpreted to them in all the Scriptures the things concerning himself" (Luke 24:27). Christ corrected their misinterpretation of the Scriptures and the recent circumstances to restore hope whereas he could have simply revealed himself to them without walking through the Scriptures. The restoration of hope came through reorienting the disciples to truth.

Similarly, Paul begins with doctrine when addressing the Thessalonians and their potential loss of hope (1 Thess 4:13–18). He even states that he does not want the Thessalonians to be "uninformed" (1 Thess 4:13), which literally means he did not want them to "not know"! He started with their thinking. A hopeless person must always start with their thinking and truth. Do they truly understand hope and what its ramifications are? Are they skewing a pseudo-biblical pseudo-worldly view of hope, which is compounding the problem? Right thinking must always precede right methodology in the restoration of hope. Point the hopeless to the God who gives his Son as Hope (Col 1:27) and gives his Word to kindle hope (Rom 15:4). Orient them to the biblical understanding of hope and then deal with the "how to's."

BATTLING HOPELESSNESS IS A COLLECTIVE EFFORT

Next, there must be a collective effort of the hopeless one facing PTSD and your family ministering to them to functionally restore hope after formally restoring hope. The hopeless must next turn to the practical steps they can take to reaffirm this hope. But might be inundated with what to do and where to begin? How does one reach up from the crevasse in which they have fallen so deeply? Richard Baxter says, "When the disease disableth them to help themselves, the most of their helps, under God, must be from others."[6] A clear understanding of hopelessness involves a collective effort in restoring hope.

How can others minister effectively to the hopeless? Richard Baxter gives some practical steps to ministering to the hopeless "As much as you can, divert them from the thoughts that are their trouble.... (3) Often set before them the great truths of the gospel

6. Baxter, "The Cure of Melancholy and Overmuch Sorrow, by Faith," 36.

that are fittest to comfort them. . . . (7) It is a useful way, if you can, to engage them in comforting others that are deeper in distresses than they."[7] There is an idea of accountability to the thoughts they are thinking and engaging them in the ministry to others, despite their own personal feelings (1 Cor 10:24; Phil 2:3). This ministry will have different facets as is true of all ministry, but those who are in a time of battling for hope with PTSD can minister to others experiencing the same phenomenon.

The first idea is that we must engage our loved one in regards to their hopeless thought patterns. We can't let them dwell on their truth, but must orient them towards God's truth. We love them enough not let them brood over their troubling thoughts. Thus we are to offer encouragement through the truths of the Scripture (Rom 15:4) and hold them accountable to those truths. You cannot let your loved one simmer in their discouraged thought patterns. You must gently and graciously enter into their despair and call them to "Hope in God" (Ps 42:5).

But in addition to their hope in God, they must be engaged in the employment of their gifts for the good of others (1 Pet 4:10; Phil 2:3–5). One of the most dangerous things is to allow our loved one suffering with PTSD, and battling hopelessness, to withdraw from meaningful service to others. Their myopic view only worsens their struggle as they focus more on their struggles than their God. This is what Baxter was suggesting: God has called us to keep ministering in our struggles. Even when our loved one is facing PTSD, we must orient them back to the truths of the gospel and meaningful service to others. This is a corporate effort and essential to their growth.

PERSONAL OBLIGATIONS OF THE HOPELESS

In addition to the much-needed counsel of others, what are the personal responsibilities of the hopeless? How do you help your loved one work through the discouraging times of PTSD? Richard

---

7. Baxter, 37–38.

Sibbes raises a good question when he poses if the hopeless should "perform duties when our hearts are altogether adverse to them."[8] Does the hopeless person need some time to "take a break" in order to rehabilitate them and cultivate hope in them? Should they take some time off so to speak? It would be arrogant to claim the following are absolute principles, without recognizing there are exceptions to every rule. There are, however, general approaches that can be taken on behalf of the one who is hopeless.

The hopeless must learn that they are required to be obedient despite their current frame of emotions (John 14:15). One of the reasons for hopelessness is often a neglect to respond biblically to their circumstances.[9] They still have to provide for their families, cut their grass, cook dinner, finish their homework, attend counseling and so forth. In an all-too-real sense, they cannot put life on hold until they "feel better." Yet at another level it might be wise to cut back *some* responsibilities so that proper attention can be placed on dealing with this hopelessness in PTSD. But where do they begin? The following are some practical steps for those hopelessly struggling with PTSD to help reorient them to the way of hope.

A good starting point would be to schedule a physical with their local physician to address any organic issues that might be exacerbating this feeling of hopelessness. They must realize that compounding problems not only refer to spiritual problems but organic problems. Dr. Robert Smith says, "Depression many times accompanies diseases, especially those of a chronic nature."[10] Although PTSD is not biological in nature, it can definitely incite a person to discouragement. Consequently, it must be taken with serious consideration if there are any organic influences into one's struggle with hopelessness, including any medications that could be intensifying negative emotions. It must be said that if there are illnesses that seem to contribute to hopelessness that the illness itself is not the *cause* of depression, as mentioned previously, but

8. Sibbes, *The Bruised Reed*, 53.

9. Cf. for further explanation of this subject: Jay Adams, *The Christian Counselor's Manual*, 378–79.

10. Smith, "A Physician Looks at Counseling: Depression," 87.

an encouragement of depression. Dr. Smith also notes, "In these cases the depression is not caused by the disease but is the reaction of the counselee to the disease."[11] A person's struggle with disease cannot be minimized at any level but cannot be maximized to the point of being deterministic. The heart is never passive, even in times of extreme physical illnesses.

After careful investigation has been completed as to any organic influences of hopelessness they should carefully move to what are their circumstances and how are they responding to them. Are they circumstantially hopeless? Their boss informed them that their colleague is receiving the promotion instead them. Are they occasionally hopeless? "I get really despondent when I am by myself." It must be carefully understood what encourages hopelessness and when does hopelessness take its flight. Some might find it a seasonal hopelessness and others a circumstantial hopelessness. However, at the root of their hopelessness, they are not responding to their circumstances biblically. Therefore, it is significant to determine which ways and in which circumstances the hopeless are responding un-biblically.

The last principle in restoring hope is drawing from the principle of putting off, being renewed, and putting on (Eph 4:22–24). It is of particular importance to this process of restoring hope. How are they responding and how should they respond biblically? The over-arching principle is that the hopeless must ask themselves, "How am I currently responding to my circumstances in a way that is not honoring to God?" Next, "How can I respond to my circumstances in a way that honors God?" This is the essence of walking by our faith, not our feelings. We want to teach the hopeless to put off the unbiblical responses and put on biblical responses to their PTSD.

In summary, what are the personal responsibilities of the hopeless? Their responsibilities are to continuously perform their God ordained duties, determine what is the will of God for them in their interaction with daily circumstances, and discern how can they obey that will. Emotions, feelings and motivations are all

11. Ibid., 87.

subjective and even peripheral to the matter of obedience to God's Word. This is a hard truth that we must present with maximum grace and compassion. It is the hopeless person's responsibility to obey these purposes and claim these promises despite their lack of desire to do so, despite their lack of hope.

THE EFFECTS OF BIBLICAL HOPE

Once biblical hope has been restored what can be expected outcomes of this hope? First and foremost it must be noted that proper biblical hope restores proper thinking. God is in control; he *is* faithful and he *does* keep his promises. Biblical hope understands this. Therefore, when biblical hope is restored, a biblical perspective is restored to our worldview. Our loved one's facing PTSD cannot find their hope in new medication, counseling methodologies, or doctors—those are not biblical forms of hope. They need robust, unshakable hope in God and his promises. They don't need to hear how medicine will stop their pain. They don't need to hear a version of, "You are going to battle this for the rest of your life but it's manageable." They need to hear that God—their Creator—has given them all things pertaining to life and godliness. And this is still true in their struggle with PTSD. They need hope. How will your family help instill that hope in them?

Chapter 7

The Mind-Life of PTSD

THE BATTLE OF PTSD is an all-too-real battle of the mind. Sure there are physiological factors that shape and influence but the heart is where those responses originate. Scripture makes it clear in Proverbs 4:23 that the issues of life originate in our hearts. Scripture also makes it clear that the heart encompasses our inner man, including our thought life (cf. Mark 7:23–24). Therefore, in order for us to minister to a person with PTSD, we must minister to their thought life (Rom 12:2). As family members, we must graciously enter into the thought life of the PTSD-sufferer in the same way that Christ graciously entered into our life.

In this chapter we are going to unpack some specific areas of thought that need intentional focus. We are to introduce a biblical understanding of suffering to the one with PTSD, reorient the nature of the traumatic event, and remove the idea of total uniqueness. It may be that you are ministering to a loved one who has great theology but poor sufferology. It may be that they are rehashing an event based on faulty observations. Or, it may be that the one with PTSD believes that they are totally unique and no one else can identify with their sufferings. All of these are false— whether intentional or not—and they need to be addressed in the mind of the one with PTSD. Let's start with a biblical understanding of suffering.

A BIBLICAL UNDERSTANDING OF SUFFERING

"*And after you have suffered a little while*, the God of all grace, who has called you to his eternal glory in Christ, will himself restore, confirm, strengthen, and establish you" (1 Pet 5:10; italics mine). Why wouldn't Peter just tell the elect exiles that it was almost done? Why not get God "off the hook"? "Hey guys, God never wanted this but soon he will make things right." Instead, Peter tells them that they need to suffer well (Ch. 2) and introduces a biblical understanding of suffering. This understanding is simply the idea of biblically understanding who God is and what he is doing through your suffering.

Peter understands suffering. In fact, he defines suffering in many ways. In his first book, he mentions suffering at least ten times to his readers and in none of the occurrences does he minimize suffering, maximize suffering, remove personal responsibility, or somehow exclude God's presence in the middle of their suffering. Rather, he says things like, "For this is a gracious thing, when, mindful of God, one endures sorrows while suffering unjustly. . . . But even if you should suffer for righteousness' sake, you will be blessed . . . for it is better to suffer for doing good, if that should be God's will" (2:20, 3:13–14). But beyond all of those affirmations of suffering and our response in suffering, we see chapter 5 verse 10: "*And after you have suffered a little while*, the God of all grace, who has called you to his eternal glory in Christ, will himself restore, confirm, strengthen, and establish you" (italics mine). " . . . Despite Christ's compassionate death for our sins, God's plan—not plan B or C or D, but his *plan*—calls for all Christians to suffer, sometimes intensely."[1] People suffering with PTSD need to know that God has a good plan in mind right in the middle of their suffering, not after their suffering, or before their suffering but in the middle of their suffering. Peter communicated this to the elect exiles and we must communicate it to our loved one with PTSD.

1. Tada and Steve Estes, *When God Weeps*, 56. This would be an excellent resource for those with a poor theology of suffering.

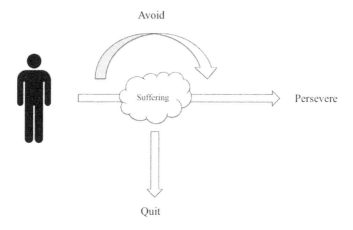

Figure 3. Responses to Suffering

But we hate suffering, no matter how good we know it can be for us; we hate it. Figure 3 represents the typical responses to suffering among people. The first response is to avoid suffering. This person, no matter what it takes, seeks to avoid suffering. When the going gets tough, they get going—going the opposite direction. They do not want life to be uncomfortable and will do what it takes, even sin, to avoid an uncomfortable situation. That avoidance stems from a poor understanding of God's abundant purposes for good even in suffering that sees comfort as supreme, not sanctification. Next are those who quit when the heat turns up. When the sayings are hard, they leave (John 6:60–66). They would stay as long as things went well but as soon as it gets difficult, they are on their way out of the door. John said they went out from us because they were not of us (1 John 2:19). The band-wagoner fan becomes evident when the season goes horrible and the band-wagoner sufferer becomes evident when the heat turns up. This is the second way in which people typically respond to suffering. "It must not be God's will because things are getting pretty tough." Or, "God closed the door" which translates into, "Things got difficult."

Lastly are those who persevere. James tells them to count it joy when they face trials and how blessed they are when they persevere in those trials (Jas 1:5, 12). Paul tells Timothy to "share in suffering as a good soldier of Jesus Christ" and he does (2 Tim 2:3). These are the people that endure hardship in ways that astounds all of us. If one word could describe their life it would be *resilient*. You can think of people whose family fractured, health deteriorated, home dilapidated, and friends dissipated but they remained faithful and persevered. They persevere in more than a, "I will try to make it" capacity. They are models for all of us to emulate because they are not the Eeyore who complains their way through suffering. No, they entrust their souls to their good Creator and seek to honor him in the midst of their pain: they persevere (1 Pet 4:19).

Arming our family members with awareness of these human tendencies will allow for effective self-counsel. They know what their predisposition will be and they know where they will be tempted. Now, the question will be how will they respond? First Peter 4:1 says, "Since therefore Christ suffered in the flesh, arm yourselves with the same way of thinking." Let's rephrase that statement: "Because Christ suffered in the flesh, be prepared to suffer like he did." Peter's words strike through our comfort and remind us of what the Lord himself said: "Remember the word that I said to you: 'A servant is not greater than his master.' If they persecuted me, they will also persecute you" (John 15:20). The person who is struggling with PTSD must believe that suffering will be part of their Christian existence. They must establish a biblical understanding of suffering.

REORIENT THEIR TRAUMATIC EVENT

One of the most helpful things you can do for your loved one is to reorient them back to truth. If you have ever participated in land navigation (and using a GPS does not count!) you are familiar with a compass, map, and a pace-count. Land navigation involves you finding a point on a map, finding where you are on the map, and then navigating yourself there in the most efficient manner. You must have a pretty good understanding of where you are and where you should be going, then you must believe that you are following the right direction to get there. There are the times of certainty, "It's just around this bend." There are also times of uncertainty, "The point should be somewhere in this area." And there are also times of absolute bewilderment: "I have no clue where I am!" Then, like a lighthouse of hope, you find a terrain feature that shows you where you are and how far until you reach your point. That terrain feature is simply a measuring point, an indicator, that you are on the right path *or* it reorients you to the right path.

In many ways you are that lighthouse of hope for your loved one who suffers from PTSD. They may think they are on the right track but are in all reality lost. You have to be the one that gently shows them where they are, where they need to go, and how they can get there. As we look at PTSD, there are three over-arching areas of bewilderment for the one suffering with PTSD: (1) guilt, (2) regret, and (3) shame.

Guilt

Guilt has many facets within a person's life and often has two, dominating manifestations. The first manifestation is the person feels guilt over what was done to them and the second manifestation is where a person has guilt over what they have done to others. We will walk through the implications of each and how to address them biblically.

First are those who are struggling with the wrongs that have been committed against them. They have a sense of guilt that what transpired was somehow their fault, they were to blame, and if they had only been more diligent certain things would not have happened to them. For instance, this is often a response of children upon finding out that their parents are getting divorced.[2] It can also be true of those who are victimized and repeatedly abused. There are thoughts that they deserve such maltreatment and other faulty ideas.

The wise family member must help orient them back towards a high view of human responsibility. Each person will be accountable

2. Tietz, "Emotions After Divorce."

for the actions that they took or did not take (Heb 9:27; cf. Ezek 18). Your family member's abuser will answer to God for his or her actions. They must see that God is intimately concerned with their suffering and he will right the wrongs committed against them (Ps 10:16–17). They must see that sins were committed against them, whether they merited them or not, their abuser should not have acted as they did. God has not called them to exact vengeance or change the past. God is with them in the present to give them grace to do what is right. As great of a person or as terrible of a person as our loved ones are, they can never *cause* another person to act sinfully. James 1 says that sin comes when we give into our sinful desires (v. 15), not when someone forces us to sin. We must remind our loved ones that everyone is responsible before God for their actions.

Next are those who feel guilt over what they have done to others. In a very real sense, their guilt is appropriate: they have sinned against another and are guilty before God. However, for others, their guilt is misguided. The first occasion is those who have truly abused, sinned against, and hurt others. They *were* wrong. Their guilt should bring what Scripture calls, "fruits of repentance" (Matt 3:8). Their guilt is a means to an end and you must grease the wheels for that motion of repentance. Paul rejoices that the Corinthian's were grieved because they were grieved into repenting (2 Cor 7:9). At this level, you can rejoice that your loved one is experiencing guilt—they should! But now you must take them to the progression of their guilt, which is to repent before God (1 John 1:8–9), and bear fruit in keeping with that repentance.

Yet in light of the above comments, we must note that some will inevitably *feel* guilty when they are not guilty before God. Where they err is in their thinking about the situation, not necessarily the actions they committed in the original situation. They may be the legalist who sees sin under every rock and need their conscience shored up with the truth of Scripture.[3] In this case, we must help show them that to sin against their conscience is a problem (Rom 14:23) but that the things they did were not innately sinful. In fact, their actions may have saved others (e.g., a soldier

---

3. Adams, *A Theology of Christian Counseling*, 146.

in combat). They must grow in their understanding to overcome this self-defeating sense of guilt for actions that could have been noble. They must believe what God says about their actions over what they say about their actions.

Most Christians who struggle with a sense of guilt often overlook the flagrant crimes committed by the apostle Paul. He admittedly was a persecutor of the church (Phil 3) and was in route to persecute other believers when Christ saved him on the road to Damascus. Yet, even the murderer of God's people can identify with these words: "There is therefore now no condemnation for those who are in Christ Jesus" (Rom 8:1). The one with PTSD must see that forgiveness is real and Christ's atoning work is sufficient. They have to trust that even if they were guilty of flagrant crimes— as was Paul—that forgiveness offered through Christ grants right standing with God. There is now no condemnation because of what Christ did for them.[4]

Regret

The second aspect of bewilderment is those who experience regret over what they did to others. The police officer who shot the criminal, the infantryman who stopped the terrorist, the pilot that dropped the missile are not guilty; they are ministers of God. Romans 13:6 tells us that these authorities are ministers of God, punishing the evildoers. This is important for a loved one to hear. They were ministers of justice, preventative grace, and an extension of God's work here on earth. They do not need to feel regret but rather gratitude; gratitude that they were able to stop evildoers before they could hurt more people; gratitude that God used them

---

4. In a very real sense, this thought of being *un*-condemned should liberate a person struggling with regret. However, reality must be noted that a person will have biological memories of circumstances in which they inflicted harm or sinned against others. Referring them back to the *Taking Your Thoughts Captive* paradigm will be of paramount importance. A person can have a biological memory come to their mind and *choose* to put the memory away through the methods described in this book; they can biblically take their thoughts captive so as to honor the Lord and grow in their walk with Christ.

to bring justice for the abused. At times, this will be an incessant self-counsel area as they wonder if they made the right decision or speculate over a million other details. The wise family member must remind them that their regrets are not founded on truth. Although this may not lessen the atrocities they witnessed, they do add value and purpose to them.

For those who are struggling with regret about sinful actions that they took, they must be reminded that their regret is not warranted if they have sought repentance through Christ. Yes, their actions are regrettable but we don't look to the things that are behind (Phil 3:13). They must deal biblically with their guilt now and then trust that God is faithful and just (1 John 1:8–9). Our loved one's regret must be put off through repentance, and they must put on greater trust that God is big enough to work through our sin to accomplish his purposes (Gen 50:20). If they wallow in their regret, they are minimizing God's forgiveness and the ability of God to work through messiness.

Shame

The temptation to feel shameful, gross, abused, and violated can be a frequent struggle of those who have been abused, especially sexually abused. Coupled with this shame is a struggle to find identity outside of this trauma that was inflicted upon them. They are not a child of God but a survivor (in their opinion). While we lament over such pain inflicted to them, we want them to see that they are new creatures if they are in Christ (2 Cor 5:17). God has caused them to become his child (John 1:12). Therefore, their shame is also unfounded. They must realize that their worth is not determined by what they or others do but only by what the infinitely wise Creator has done, namely adopting them into his family.[5] Their identity in Christ will overpower their shame as they bask in God's work in their life.

5. Jerry Bridges has provided an excellent resource entitled, *Who Am I? Identity in Christ*, that will serve as an excellent resource to the one experiencing shame.

Their shame should be evaluated to see if it is true, biblical guilt. If it is then the Bible calls them to repentance and change (1 John 1:8–10). However, if there is no guilt from the shame that they are experiencing, that shame must be put off and they must think God's thoughts about their circumstances and themselves. Shame is not self-determined, meaning we don't pick over what to be shameful. Shame is a gift of God that leads us to repentance. When one seeks to cling to shame in truly un-shameful situations it indicates pride, not an authentically sensitive nature. The reason it indicates pride is because God has not called what they experienced as something to be shameful. Therefore, to make it shameful is to overstep the boundaries of what God has prescribed. Your loved one with PTSD must be willing to see their shame as God sees it, and approach it with the remedies that he provides.

TRAUMA IS NUANCED BUT NOT UNIQUE

This section is one of the most delicate components of ministering to the one with PTSD. It seethes with a potential callousness that should terrify us. The principle is this: a person's trauma is not unique in that others can identify and understand what they have experienced. 1 Corinthians 10:13 says, "No temptation has overtaken you *that is not common to man.* God is faithful, and he will not let you be tempted beyond your ability, but with the temptation he will also provide the way of escape, that you may be able to endure it" (emphasis added). Their fight with PTSD will seem entirely alien to those who were not there, have not experienced what they experienced, and seemingly cannot relate. *However, this is not true.*

Some will cling to this thought intentionally and others unintentionally, but as a family member you must reorient them to proper thinking about their trauma. God has promised that no temptation that they have experienced is totally unique to them. This should break down the barriers of a, "how would you know?" mentality; a temptation that some sufferers of PTSD will experience. They will question another person's ability to help because they were not there, they did not experience what they experienced, so how could they know? What is being revealed in those movements is an exclusivist pride. "I will not listen to you—or anyone else—because you cannot know the pain I endured."

At one level you cannot know the pain—nor should you. You do not need to experience a divorce to know the pain it causes on a family. You do not have to be in a firefight to understand its dangers. You may never fully understand what they experienced but you can take them to the man of sorrows who was acquainted with grief (Isa 53). You can show them that Christ is the only true victim in the history of mankind and that he endured patiently and never sinned when he was traumatized (1 Pet 2:18–25). *He* can identify with them and wants to identify with them (Heb 4:15–16). Therefore, do not engage in a comparison of whose suffering was worse by way of establishing credibility. Or, on the other hand, do not let your relatively pain-free life prevent you from ministering to them during their time of great suffering. Rather, empathize with them as you take them to the One who knows their every struggle and beckons them to cast their cares on him (1 Pet 5:7), while praying for wisdom to be sensitive and compassionate.

The wise family member is the beacon of hope, the bearer of good news. That good news is none other than the Gospel. And it is the Gospel that will reorient your loved one back on track. God has brought this PTSD into their life for their good and is working greater Christlikeness out of this on their behalf. They may be veering or absolutely lost in their navigation through the terrain of life, so you must gently walk with them and guide them. This idea sets the stage for our next chapter, which will discuss orienting your family for this type of ministry.

Chapter 8

Orienting Your Family for Ministry

YOUR FAMILY IS THE CONTEXT FOR MINISTRY

Part of the desire of your family should to be to engineer your family's structure to minister towards the nuances of your loved one with PTSD. This does not mean that a family now is PTSD centered, rather than God-centered. What it means is that in the same way your family would adapt for any other form of suffering, they should also adapt for one suffering from PTSD.

TUGBOATS AND MINISTRY

Tugboats are inglorious; they are rugged, somewhat ugly, and by no means a luxury-liner. But despite their ingloriousness, the purpose of tugboats is very important: their purpose is to help the vessels that cannot move or those vessels that should not move. At times a tugboat moves an oversized vessel that should not move through a narrow canal because of the damage it will cause to other vessels, docks, and miscellaneous items nearby. At other times a tugboat's task is to tow disabled vessels, ones that have broken down and need to be pushed or pulled through rivers, oceans, and canals. The tugboat will escort the disabled vessel to a safe place so it can be repaired. The tugboat is not a speedboat, although there are tugboat races. It is not a cruise liner or a yacht; it is a small inglorious but necessary boat.

The tugboat provides a great illustration for parakaleō ministry. Parakaleō ministry is derived from the ministry of the second Paraclete and has much to do with helping broken, sinful people find restoration, even if that means pushing at times and pulling at other times. In parakaleō ministry, we help those who cannot move and those who should not move. We come along side of them and minister to them to prevent further damage to themselves or anyone else. We are the tugboat family member that has an inglorious job at times but is there to minister no matter the level of glory. Therefore, it is the purpose of this chapter to show that the ministry of the second Paraclete, the Holy Spirit, offers an excellent model for ministry. I want to show you this by observing the Holy Spirit's ministry to believers and drawing out the implications for our ministry to our family.

A MODEL FOR MINISTRY

There is one primary passage that introduces the idea of a Paraclete coming to minister to believers: the upper room discourse. In this section we have some phenomenal events that unfold. Some of which are when Jesus takes it upon himself to wash the feet of his disciples (13:1–20), he identifies the mole among his disciples (13:21–30), restates the importance of loving others as he is on the brink of death (13:31–35), and teaches about the "Helper" that will take his place (14:16, 26, 16:4b–11). Jesus introduces an idea that has been recorded in no other Gospel and that idea is that there will be *another* Helper coming. Although this would not be totally foreign to the disciples (as we will discuss later), this is the first time that the Gospel narratives show us this promise from Jesus.

It is important to note the terminology that Jesus uses in John 14. Look at verses 16–17: "And I will ask the Father, and he will give you *another Helper*, to be with you forever, even the *Spirit of truth*, whom the world cannot receive, because it neither sees him nor knows him" (emphasis added). Jesus is stating that there are in fact two Helpers: he is one Helper and the Holy Spirit—who is coming—is the other Helper.

In John's epistle he tells us that even if you sin as a believer, you have an Advocate with the Father (1 John 2:1); that Advocate is none other that the Son of God, "Jesus Christ the righteous" (1 John 2:1). The weight of this statement was intended to bring great peace to the disciples as they first heard these new words. "Peace I leave with you; my peace I give to you" (14:27). The disciples were to feel the great relief that they were not to be abandoned when Jesus, the first Paraclete, left. Someone else was coming and that new Helper would minister to believers as Jesus ministered to them. In fact, Jesus said it is advantageous to the disciples for him to go away because that means the Helper would come; the second Helper is good news! Because the second Helper is good news the disciples had reason for peace and for rejoicing.

Christ tells of another *Helper* promised but what exactly does that mean? The term literally means "one who is called to someone's aid."[1] It has vivid imagery of the Holy Spirit's answer to the call of the Father to send him to believers. So in one aspect, the term *Helper* accurately represents the original word but there is one more aspect of *Helper*, namely the aspect of an advocate.

As mentioned above, Jesus is described as the Advocate of the believer who sins (1 John 2:1). The advocate conjures up thoughts of a courtroom where a trial is taking place and the advocate is speaking, interceding, and representing a defendant.[2] In John's Gospel, he uses the same type courtroom setting to show the work of the second Paraclete (16:8–11).

Without being obvious, it is important to note that the Holy Spirit is called the Helper because he comes to intercede, represent, walk alongside of, advocate, and to aid. He comes to help and he succeeds in that mission! The ministry implications for this are

1. Arndt, Danker, and Bauer, *A Greek-English Lexicon of the New Testament*, s.v. "παράκλητος."

2. Kittel, Bromiley, and Friedrich, *Theological Dictionary of the New Testament*, 803.

massive and we will begin to unpack some of those implications by considering the various aspects of both Paraclete ministries. The over-arching aspects of ministry are that we will see the Paraclete offer a faithful presence, teaching, bearing witness of Jesus, and advocacy.

ASPECTS OF BOTH PARACLETES MINISTRIES

The Ministry of Faithful Presence

The first comfort that Jesus promises to the disciples is that the next Paraclete will be "with you forever . . . [and] you know him for he dwells with you and will be in you" (John 14:16, 17). One of most comforting commands given throughout the Scripture is that God will be with us. This is a consistent teaching throughout the Bible: God is with his people (cf. Gen 28:15; Deut 31:6–8; 1 Chr 28:20; Matt 28:20; Heb 13:5). Why is it so important that we hear that God is with us or with your loved one through the struggle of PTSD? In almost every case there is a fear that is being addressed: new leadership, worry of money, Jesus is now gone, and Solomon newly instated. God said to Joshua, "Do not be frightened, and do not be dismayed, *for the Lord your God is with you* wherever you go" (Deut 1:9; italics mine). The cure to fear is the recognition that God is with us, which is exactly what Christ promises to the disciples. God, the Holy Spirit, is with them.

The promise of the Holy Spirit and the promise of God's presence translate very pointedly into the ministry context with your loved one. How will you be present for your family member? The method of the second Paraclete is an *abiding* presence, one that stays with a believer. How will you minister faithfully to your family member? Are you in a rush to "fix them" and send them on their way so you can get back to life as normal? The ministry of the Holy Spirit is one that abides and resides with us. He does not stick around just long enough to say he came but his ministry is one of continual accompaniment. A loving family member must be willing to minister with longevity.

One other implication is that of presence *only*. As a family member we have a tendency to rush into a circumstance and begin instructing. The presence of the Holy Spirit teaches us that ministering to people can come through the ministry of presence. Yes, instruction is necessary and will be required but pull back on the reigns before you begin to hand it out to your family member. We see this with Job's friends in the Old Testament and a few people in the New Testament. Job's friends sat for days in silence with Job before they began to wax eloquent. Onesimus and Epaphroditus are two characters in the New Testament that embody the ministry of presence. The Scripture never states any instruction that they gave to Paul but only that they both ministered to Paul in a time of need through their presence. This is important to note: it was not their words that were so helpful to Paul but their presence. As a family member of one with PTSD, you can incarnate some of the teachings that you want your loved one to understand. In this way the ministry of presence exceeds any words that you can communicate to your family member.

The Ministry of Instruction

The second ministry of the Holy Spirit as provided in John's gospel is one of instruction. John 14:26 says, "But the Helper, the Holy Spirit, whom the Father will send in my name, *he will teach you all things*" (italics mine). Other passages in the Gospel of John point to the disciples understanding something only after Christ had risen from the dead (2:19–22, 12:16, 20:9), which is exactly what Christ promised would happen when he ascended (14:26). In the immediate context, Jesus was referring to the first disciples as the ones whom the Holy Spirit would personally instruct.

However, the Holy Spirit did teach and instruct those first disciples by reminding them of what Christ previously said; he instructed them. The model of parakaleō ministry is one of gentle instruction (2 Tim 2:25). This must not be overlooked or minimized. The tendency of man is towards either grace or truth as

Randy Alcorn so helpfully articulated.[3] Yet the biblical solution is found in the balance of grace *and* truth. The Holy Spirit not only ministers in presence but also in instruction. We will discuss the content of instruction in greater detail later in the book, but suffice it for now to observe that instruction is a part of the Holy Spirit's ministry to the early disciples. Thus, you should be willing to offer instruction to your loved one. Don't jump to instruction without a ministry of presence to them, but note that with their struggle in facing PTSD they need to hear biblical instruction.

The Ministry of Bearing Witness

Moreover, the Holy Spirit is in no way a rogue member of the Trinity teaching his own doctrine and presenting his own ideas. The relationship of the Trinity is beautifully portrayed in John 15:26: "But when the Helper comes, whom I will send to you from the Father, the Spirit of truth, who proceeds from the Father, he will bear witness about me." Every person of the Trinity is shown in this statement and another aspect of the Holy Spirit: "He will bear witness about me" (15:26).

Jesus states in the future tense, that the Holy Spirit would bear witness about him. This *witness* is testifying who Christ is and what he has done. Of all of the New Testament books, John uses this terminology more than any other author. He refers to John the Baptist as bearing witness (John 1:32), Jesus' works bear witness about him (5:36), and the Father bears witness about Jesus (8:18). The concept is that the Holy Spirit will speak to the world about Christ in the same way that the disciples will bear witness about Christ (15:27).

Likewise it must be noted that all helpful ministry goes back to Christ; how can it not? The person with PTSD needs to hear that God is intimately concerned with their struggles and has reached out to them through the work of Christ. The wife who has been left behind by her husband needs to know that Christ will never leave

3. Alcorn, *The Grace and Truth Paradox.*

her. The child who was abused by their parents needs to know that Christ is going to set things straight—vengeance is not their own. In emulating the Holy Spirit through parakaleō ministry, the family member must never forget that the gospel is of first importance: the story about Christ (1 Cor 15:1–3). In every context they must be thinking how the Gospel relates to that person's problems and how that person relates to the Gospel. We must bear witness to the work of Christ when ministering to our loved one's with PTSD.

The Ministry of Advocacy

Advocacy[4] is often a term that Westerner's will associate with one person helping another to fight for justice: advocate of the underprivileged, the inner city kid, the homeless mom, the recently disabled father, whomever. These are all situations that conjure up advocacy in our modern thinking. However, in 1 John 2:1 we have another layer of advocacy that Jesus represents. Listen to these words: "My little children, I am writing these things to you so that you may not sin. But if anyone does sin, we have an advocate with the Father, Jesus Christ the righteous."

The irony of our Western thinking is that we envision an advocate coming to the aid of a *guiltless* person: the orphan, the widow, or the abused. When John speaks of Christ's work as an advocate, he does so with the perspective of Jesus coming to the aid of *guilty* people: the murderer, the felon, the wife-beater, and the crook. "In the present context, . . . [Advocate] undoubtedly signifies a legal advocate or counsel for the defense."[5] Christ is in a very robust sense, our defense attorney. We are criminal defendants who stand before a God—the righteous Judge (Gen 7:11)—and we are infinitely guilty of the most heinous of crimes. Yet, our defense attorney has entered into our world and advocated on our behalf before a righteous Judge. That is the profound mystery of the Gos-

---

4. For a good discussion on some of the various facets of advocacy, refer to Appendix B of Ken Sande's *The Peacemaker*, 270–275.

5. Rogers Jr., and Rogers III, *The New Linguistic and Exegetical Key to the Greek New Testament*, 592.

pel; namely, our defense attorney absorbed our punishment and imputed to us his innocence.

But packed into the middle of this vibrant analogy is again more ministry implications. The wise family member must be an advocate for their loved ones, *even* their guilty loved ones. Yes, we want to be the Robin Hood-type family member who is dealing justice and correcting corruption but do we mourn with the consistently poor decision maker? Do we weep with the abuser? Do we feel sorrow for the pregnant teen mom? Do we grieve over the misfortunes of sinners who made sinful decisions? At one level, it can be natural for us to think of our family members: "that is what you get! If you did not do x then y would not have happened." But at another level, that thinking is totally unbiblical. Rather we should resound with the thought that if it were not for the grace of God, we too would be making such terrible decisions!

Imagine that God took the same posture as we do: "That is what you get. I told you. Now you get a taste of your own medicine." What a tragedy—for us! On the contrary, parakaleō ministry—in emulating the first Paraclete—identifies with guilty people and helps them sort through the mess *they* have created. In the same way that Christ helps us sort through our own sin mess, the wise family member can help others sort through their sin mess. There does not need to be a condemning tone of "I told you so" but a rather sweet embodiment of truth that says, "You were wrong but I am here to help. I am *your* advocate by representing the true Advocate."

As you can see, the standard set by the Holy Spirit's ministry to believers provides an excellent template of ministry to others— especially those facing PTSD. We want to orient our families so that we see presence as part of our ministry. We don't have to wax eloquent with long sermons on God's plans, but often we just need to be there. And in being there, we will need to offer instruction. Presence without instruction, it form without substance.

In addition, we recognize that the entire orientation of our family's ministry must be towards Christ. We are also to bear witness of him. Our ministry is from him, through him, and to him (Rom 11:36). We do this ministry as advocates, even of guilty family members. We do it because that is what Christ has done for us. May we do so with loving graciousness and faithful perseverance as we look to the day when we will be united with the first Paraclete for eternity! May our families be oriented towards parakaleō ministry for the long haul!

Chapter 9

Practical Steps for Family Ministry

PARAKALEŌ MINISTRY IS ALMOST a paradigm by which to view your family's ministry, therefore this next chapter is going to provide a blueprint of specific steps for implementing change. It would only be mildly helpful to tell a family that they need to offer a ministry of presence to their loved one without showing them what that ministry should look like with some details. But it would also be unhelpful for a person to jump strait to the details yet omit the development of a paradigm for their ministry: both are necessary and in a progressive manner. When we understand the biblical call for presence, advocacy, bearing witness, and instruction, then we then can implement specific steps for ministry. Moreover, these specific steps for ministry begin with understanding.

UNDERSTANDING THEIR STRUGGLES AND WEAKNESSES

One of your family's first goals is to understand.[1] *All effective ministry happens in the context of understanding* (Prov 18:2, 13); re-

---

1. One of the best things a family can do is to study the process of biblical change as they seek to walk their loved one through that process. Ephesians 4:22–24 enumerates that process with the overarching principles of "putting off, being renewed in the spirit of your minds, and putting on the new self."

member this. Your family needs to watch what triggers flashbacks, negative thinking, irritability, and anger. What circumstances seem to be difficult for them? Is it car rides? Is it large crowds? What really sets off your loved one or what really tempts them towards PTSD symptoms? Look and listen. You have a story line unfolding before your eyes and only when you take the time to observe and note what are the struggles and weaknesses of your family member, can you help them. They are not a walking diagnosis or a personification of the DSM; they are real people with idiosyncrasies. Ask them, watch their responses, and seek to understand what times are so difficult for them in their struggle. Really, you must understand their struggle if you are going to be able to help them grow and change: "if one gives and answer before he hears, it is folly and shame" (Prov 18:13).

EXHIBITING DEMANDING PATIENCE

Paul Tripp expresses an importance concept when he says, "The grace that adopts me into Christ's family is not a grace that says I am okay. In fact, the Bible is clear that God extends his grace to me because I am everything *but* okay."[2] We must exhibit the demanding patience that Christ exhibits towards us. We endure, we forbear, we are longsuffering but we seek growth—true growth. This growth is none other than a willingness to submit to the will of God and his purposes for their life (Phil 1:6). God has started something in their life if they are a believer and he has promised change will happen: they must be growing into the image of Christ. Remember that there is no 'timeline' for recovery and recovery is not the goal: honoring God is the goal and growth into the image of Christ is the goal. Do not measure their progress by how much they struggled with PTSD a year ago but by their growth in Christ. Your patience should be a patience that calls them to growth, only then is it a loving patience.

Also cf. Jim Berg's "Understanding Biblical Change" in *Changed Into His Image: God's Plan for Transforming Your Life*.

2. Tripp, *Instruments in the Redeemer's Hands*, 158.

MEDICAL DOCTORS ARE A MUST

Seek out the help of a wise medical doctor initially, preferably a Christian medical doctor. You will need their insights to help observe biological influences to your loved one with PTSD. While the Bible never teaches a deterministic model of biology, it does recognize the strong relationship between the inner man and the outer man (Ps 51). Therefore, we do not want to minimize that relationship either.

In addition to a medical doctor, seek to speak with a nutritionist and a sleep specialist. There are often vast improvements for people who simply practice good nutrition and ensure that they are resting adequately. These are both biblical ideas of stewarding our bodies as temples in which the Holy Spirit dwells and they are very wise to consider (1 Cor 6:19–20). A typical symptom of PTSD is hyper-agitation that prevents good sleep therefore insomnia ensues. Once insomnia has set in, there will be a compounding effect of the symptoms of PTSD. Therefore, preventative nutrition is very ideal, even if this means some type of sleep aid. Remember that stewarding the outer man well has huge influences on the inner man (1 Tim 5:23).

But whether or not you do visit a nutritionist or sleep specialist, you must be extremely mindful of sleep patterns. If your loved one is not sleeping enough, you will have to intervene very quickly. Insomnia is one of the dominant characteristics of PTSD and it is a very real and dangerous aspect of PTSD. You cannot take insomnia flippantly or lightly. Therefore, be cognizant of their sleep patterns. Note how many hours they are sleeping within the context of how many they would sleep before. If necessary, log their hours for your own records but keep a watchful eye to ensure that your loved one is getting the proper amount of rest.

If they are not resting well then consider a myriad of factors: how much caffeine are they eating or drinking? How close to bedtime are they eating? Are they watching television or searching the Internet right up to bedtime? How are they winding down a part of each day? Some of these unknown habits are contributing to their sleeplessness and need to be discarded until your loved one has established proper sleep patterns. The principle is, though, take into consideration biological influences and be proactive with nutrition and sleep.

CONDUCIVE ENVIRONMENTS FOR CHANGE

Circumstances

We recognize that our circumstances don't cause us to sin. Joseph and Daniel illustrate this in the Scriptures (Gen 45–50; Dan 1). However, environments do have an influence upon us and should be taken into consideration (1 Cor 15:33). In the beginning of your ministry to your loved one with PTSD it will be imperative to avoid circumstances that trigger flashbacks. You will want to identify what circumstances trigger PTSD symptoms and seek to *contain* exposure to them as best as possible. It would be terribly inconsiderate to constantly expose a person to circumstances that conjure up symptoms of PTSD. Yet, it would be equally terrible to never expose them to the circumstances that plague their memories.

Moreover, certain circumstances cannot or should not be avoided. For instance, one individual suffered with painful memories of a childhood that was extremely abusive—both physically and sexually.[3] Her flashbacks were typically triggered when she would enter the kitchen or take a shower, which are both places that she had to visit. Therefore, the counselor could not tell her to avoid these places but rather to *observe* the patterns of her flashbacks and how they relate to these places. Do these places or circumstances conjure up the painful memory and what about the circumstance does this? Is it a smell, the lights, the noise level, or the people? What associates this place with the place that your painful memory occurred? Once you have connected this dot, then you can wisely approach a plan of thinking and doing, principles of being a truth-thinker, and other related efforts that orient your loved one back to reality.

For the circumstances that you can avoid (e.g., the market, the home, the woods, etc.) seek to wisely abstain from visiting these

3. Lambert, *Hard Cases*, 39.

locations at first. You will want to counsel and disciple your loved one in preparation for visiting such places or types of circumstances. Secular psychology would term this *exposure therapy* but it is nothing more than wisely and lovingly introducing the circumstances that stimulate the painful memories of a person's past. Your goal is to teach them how to approach these circumstances and then to by faith live out that instruction in the midst of their difficult environment.

Yet the aim is not behavior modification. Behavior modifications says, "Avoid those type of circumstances and all is well." However, true and authentic heart change orients itself towards God's purposes in the middle of those environments. For example, to avoid a place with a large crowd may be wise initially but through the power of the Holy Spirit, a person can learn to trust God and believe he will not leave them *even* in large groups (Heb 13:5). There is an enormous importance in being wisely reintroduced to environments that stimulate those painful feelings so a person can grow in those regards. To avoid the circumstance completely is only wise in a few instances and behavior modification in most instances.

One last thought in this context is to understand that God has promised to give every believer all that they need to respond in a godly way in their trials (1 Cor 10:13). This means for our loved ones with PTSD, they will not be put in a circumstance by the Providence of God in which they cannot control their response. God is with them; he will give them grace to do what is right. They can walk by faith in their circumstances that encourage them towards PTSD symptoms (2 Cor 5:7) knowing that God is using these circumstances to refine their faith.

Avoid Known Stimuli

Out of the same vein, recognize the stimuli in a person's life. If you know that a person struggles in a loud environment (as most with PTSD will do) then seek to keep the noise down. This is a manifestation of the golden rule (Luke 6:31) and Philippians 2:2–5; consider their interests as more important or simply how you would want to be treated. Be careful not to slam the door or play a certain song. Ensure that you do not yell in the house or touch them in a certain way. The idea is that you know these stimuli so as not to tempt or incite painful memories unnecessarily. Here are some questions that could be helpful in identifying these stimuli:

1. When do episodes tend to flare up? Is there a certain time of the day? Is there a certain event? Is there a certain context? Were you inside or outside? Was it close to a mealtime?

2. What was happening? What were you doing? What were they doing? What were others doing around them (i.e., the kids running around the living room)?

3. Where were you? Were you at home? On a car ride? In a shop? Eating out?

4. How was the person acting before? Were they tired? Were they irritable? Were they distant? Were they brooding? Were they in deep thought? Were they manic? What was the person acting like before the symptoms started again?

These types of questions can easily be logged so you can look for themes within your loved one. And in a very real sense, you may observe what they do not. They may not see that when they are hungry they are more susceptible to flashbacks. They may not notice that when they are in deep thought with much free time, they have more flashbacks. These areas will be very important as you seek to understand your loved one and help them grow in their walk with Christ.

A warning is necessary here: even though a person may have a certain stimuli now does not mean they are sanctioned for ungodliness and unrighteous responses. Be gentle and gracious here by not exacerbating them but also calling them to grow in this area. For instance, if your spouse really struggles to be calm and control their anger when the kids are yelling in the house, there is a two-fold obligation. The first is to address the kids and call them to be kind, considerate, and die to their own desires to be loud and rambunctious. Next, there is an obligation to call your spouse to grow in this area.[4] Even though the kids are screaming like wild banshees, your spouse have an obligation to honor God in that moment.

Identify Accountability

One of the common associations of PTSD is domestic violence, especially for military members suffering from PTSD. There is much research that needs to be conducted as to why certain demographics are more prone to violence than others but do note that violence may be an issue that you need to consider. Part of that consideration is who to call alongside of your family for help. At this point, you would identify someone who can hold your loved one accountable (Jas 5:16). One of the most practical ways is for your loved one to pick the accountability partner (AP). You can simply say, "I'd like you to pick someone we can call if you get into a heated moment." This allows for your loved one to make that choice, and pick someone they respect and would also give them wise, biblical counsel.

An AP is simply a Christian who will help to implement in daily living biblical instruction and biblical confrontation (Gal 6:1–3). In the instance of one struggling with PTSD, it is extremely helpful to identify a person who could also function as an accountability partner. This AP would function so as to be on call for help with our loved one. For instance, if your husband is having flashbacks again and now his anger is quickly escalating and he is threatening, hitting walls, and throwing things, it would be a good time to call the accountability partner. The presence of another person who is outside of the immediate family will have cooling effects to the circumstance but also can help protect all of those involved. It also allows for that accountability partner to reinforce what you have been saying, while ensuring that you are not contributing to the problem, too (Prov 18:17).

---

4. This may also be a great opportunity for the family member to show their loved one the biblical teaching that a person's circumstances does not determine their heart attitude but only reveals their heart attitude (Prov 4:23; Mark 7:21–23).

One of the over-arching reasons that this is so important is because when the police get involved in familial conflict, there is no undoing what has been done. Father's will go to jail, Child Protective Services will start investigations, and criminal records are now created. The permanency of involving the police—although necessary at times—may not be the best solution. It is important to have a godly AP who will lovingly confront, minister to, and encourage (Gal 6:1–3; Eph 4:15). While the accountability partner may still contact police, it at least offers a wise third-party that can be a help in conflict resolution. Whatever their role, let the AP minister to your loved one when times get difficult.

Avoid Significant Free Times

Because PTSD is very much a battle of a person's thought life, be careful to ration free time well. Meaning, look at the hours in a day and see where the gaps are in your loved one's schedule. Ephesians 5:16 applies to them, so help them make the most of their time. When are they going to have gobs of free time? When will they be prone towards introspection? Seek to positively engage those times and fill them with fruitful and helpful things. Start new hobbies, seek out new opportunities to serve the church, find some books that would be great to read, exercise, invite friends over for dinner, and other ways that will be a fruitful way of engaging this free time. Make the most of their time to the glory of God (Col 4:5; 1 Cor 10:31)!

The idea is that they will not have the time to sit around and rehash the painful memories. While this is not an end in itself, it is a very appropriate means to an end. In fact, introspection must be done in proportion for all of us, not only those suffering with PTSD. So guard their time well as you help to shepherd their thought life.

Fulfill Daily Responsibilities

One of the chief concerns you should have with your loved one is whether or not they are completing their daily responsibilities (Matt 25:23). Are they being faithful to what God has given them to do? Are they going to work on time? Are they going to school? Are they completing the responsibilities they have? Some of this will tie back into helping manage their free time but also seek to ensure that their responsibilities are being fulfilled. Employers will only be gracious for so long. Schools will only be gracious for so long. If your loved one is consistently failing to fulfill their responsibilities it will snowball into a very difficult situation quickly. They must learn to be truth-led, as we discussed above. There will be many days during which they don't feel like fulfilling their responsibilities. However, by faith they must do so.

Moreover, be willing to 'check-in' on them. This is not a mild form of stalking but rather a form of accountability. Things like going by their work to drop off a surprise coffee or asking them if you can come eat with them at lunch break. Taking them to work and picking them up. Going by their house and helping with some of the chores and also reviewing homework and contacting teachers to ensure that your loved one is fulfilling their obligations. The best policy is to be very straightforward with your loved one and tell them that you want to serve them and help ensure that they are fulfilling their obligations, whether they want you to or not. You do not want to breach their trust in an attempt to serve them but can be very candid as to why you would like to serve them in this way. And even if they would prefer that you not come by their work or school, be creative and wise as to how you can fulfill that intent in a different manner (e.g., ask a co-worker, look at pay stubs, et cetera).

The principle is, however, that they must be fulfilling their daily responsibilities even in the middle of their struggles with PTSD. God has provided sufficient grace to do so and to neglect their responsibilities is only going to make matters worse. Your close accountability may seem like police work initially but it just might prevent the downward spiral of PTSD to the worsening of PTSD by irresponsibility.

Helping Children

Children who have suffered greatly in terms of experiencing trauma are, in most instances, going to be extraordinarily sensitive and vulnerable. One child might take a more reclusive posture and withdraw from everyone and the other child might cling to anyone that has a pulse. If your family has a child experiencing PTSD then you must be diligent to pursue them. Do not let the barriers, the outbursts, or the random and bizarre behavior discourage you; they need your persistent—parakaleō-esque—presence in their life. You as the guardian must also ensure a few things are taking place for your child. At a minimum, you must provide regularity/consistency for them and provide overt amounts of safety.

The child who has been victimized needs regularity. *Please do not miss this point: your child needs regularity.* This means that bedtime, waking time, meal times, school times, and down times are very regimented. As you are seeking to build an environment that is conducive for change and growth, you must have a very regimented schedule. Your child does not need to be disoriented by the chaos of their schedule. If this means that you quit Boy Scouts, then please quite boy scouts (at least for a time). Your priority should be to provide a regular schedule for your child.

Another aspect of regularity is who will be watching your child. In a best-case scenario, the guardian(s) will have the bulk of the time with their child. This means they are the ones picking them up from school, taking them to school, tucking them in at night, helping with homework and every other detail of your kid's day. If the guardian cannot be the primary one who is keeping the child, then you must ensure that whomever is keeping them is doing so on a *regular basis.* Meaning, try to avoid one person watching the child one day, another person the next day, another the next day and so on. By having a consistent caretaker, it will greatly contribute to a sense of security and allow you to help your child respond to their trauma and grow in greater Christlikeness. If you are using a babysitter or nanny, ensure that you are communicating with them regularly and incorporating some type of thorough 'debrief' before and after they take over.

In that time of debrief, be very straightforward with your caretaker as to your expectations, there is no room for miscommunication or assumptions. Therefore, you should tell them that you want them to be fully engaged in your child in your absence. This means that there should not be a response like, "They spent most of the day in their room." You also want them to be very observant of your child's behaviors and emotions. Did they get upset? Did they seem withdrawn? Did they seem 'normal'? Some guardians may use an observation log or some type of way for a caretaker (especially those who will have them for entire days) to journal observations about their child. The idea is that you can provide accountability and observation even if you are not physically present with your child. If your caretaker is not able (or willing) to commit to this detailed level of *care-taking*, then do your best to find someone else, especially at first.

The guiding thought behind regularity is that your child would know what to expect, even if you did not tell them what was happening next. Meaning, if it is Thursday and they are getting home from school, they already know what to expect for that evening and also who will be with them that evening. This level of regularity will greatly increase your ability to minister to your child and help them grow through this difficult time.

Another aspect of ministering to your child is to ensure that you are exhibiting overt measures to ensure your child's safety and sense of security. This is not implying that your house must be covered in bubble wrap and fumigated with Lysol but that you are ultra-cognizant of their safety and *sense* of security. You should consider practical ways to help them know they are safe while pointing them to ultimate safety in God (Ps 56:3). Things like a split sleeping schedule with the guardians sleeping in their room,[5]

5. A specific plan for addressing night terrors or nightmares will be very beneficial to your family. In order to prevent regular chaos in your home by disrupting everyone's sleep on a regular basis you must think through and pray through how you can best serve your child in their nightmares/night terrors. A few considerations are to: (1) make a plan on how to safely wake them up; (2) plan for de-escalating them and reorienting them to reality as discussed in chapter 4 (e.g., music, back rubs, reading to them); (3) praying with them and

picking them up from school and taking them to school, avoid leaving them alone initially, and quickly confront any abusive/bullying behavior by peers and siblings. You are not seeking to create a bubble by which you are shielding them from the messiness of life because they will one day encounter this mess. Rather, you are seeking—for a time—to foster an environment that is conducive to biblical change (e.g., greater Christlikeness in their life). Consequently, if your child is in constant upheaval and does not know whom to trust, you are stoking the fire rather than putting it out.

Logically, most people will also want an answer to the next thought: "How long should we be willing or seek to implement this level of care?" A short answer: plan for months, not years. Think in terms of growth and discipleship. During this time of extremely vigilant[6] care taking, seek to wean them off of this level of support. Their growth should involve a greater reliance on their true Rock and refuge (Ps 18:2) not on how well you can engineer their circumstances to prevent PTSD symptoms. Moreover, avoid the temptation to be their functional savior, as natural as it may seem at times; it will only worsen your child's struggles and stymie their growth. Christ is their Savior, not you. However, you should seek to provide wise, stable and regulated environments in which your child is generally safe.

---

reminding them of the promises of God; (4) helping them put on God-honoring responses to their nightmares (e.g., singing to them/with them, memorizing Scripture that will fit this context, thanking God for certain things in their life); (5) lastly, determine beforehand who will minister to them during these times. It is not necessary for the entire house to wake-up for hours every night as that will only exacerbate the problem rather than help in the long-term.

6. In this section I'm not seeking to imply that parents or guardians of all children are not to exhibit a level of hyper-vigilance. On the other hand, I am seeking to communicate that the *expression* of that diligence is manifested more overtly. For instance, a split-sleep schedule would be detrimental to most kids (and marital relationships!) but for those kids with PTSD, it can be an integral part of ensuring the child sleeps well, avoids nightmares/flashbacks as best as possible, and knows that they can rely on their parents/guardians in the midst of their fears.

MAINTAINING A REDEMPTIVE POSTURE

It is possible to minister to your loved ones in a functionally atheistic manner. Functionally atheistic in that there is no thought of God in their trials, no thought of how he is using this trial to make them more like Christ, no thought of how can they serve others in their trials, or no thought of how they can rejoice in their sufferings. This sort of ministry is well intended but functionally atheistic and extremely detrimental. Secular psychologies will want to lump your loved one into a category of PTSD—the end. No hope; only medication; maybe time will heal all wounds. What is missing from that equation? God! God is missing from the equation and no matter how astute the observations on what your loved one is experiencing, secular psychology cannot thoroughly address *how* they should experience it. Therefore, your family must maintain a redemptive posture.

A redemptive posture, first of all, does not see relief as the goal of its ministry; it sees greater Christlikeness as the goal. Feel the weight of this observation for just a moment more: your goal is not to remove suffering, minimize suffering, or ignore suffer but rather to *contextualize* suffering. A redemptive posture sees that suffering should lead to greater Christlikeness (1 Pet 2–3; Jas 1:5; Rom 8:29–29) and if that is true, then we should not avoid it but welcome it. The person with PTSD needs to see their struggle as suffering so they can connect the dots to how God requires them to respond (cf. Chapter 7). Consequently, they need to know that even if they continue to have flashbacks for the rest of their lives, they can honor God in their suffering. Therefore, relief is not the goal in a redemptive posture but rather greater Christlikeness.

In addition, engineering circumstances in not intended to be a functional savior, but rather a conduit of reliance on God and the Holy Spirit to change. If we are not careful, these ways of ministering become demands that never will dissipate but will promote the ongoing effects of PTSD. As mentioned above, your family is seeking to create an environment that is conducive for change. Therefore, it must be noted, a family can create an environment that is an incubator for PTSD to grow. If your family creates an environment for change, the inference is that change needs to happen—true change, not circumstantial change. You are exhibiting demanding patience in your redemptive posture but removing your family's PTSD 'training wheels' of sorts. To keep the circumstances—the training wheels—in place for too long will only inhibit the person's long-term growth.

One last aspect of a redemptive posture is to recognize and applaud the growth of your loved one. Whether it is a child who now sleeps through the night or an adult who is starting to self-counsel really well, note their growth. This will have a two-fold effect: (1) they will see how the Lord is working in their suffering and (2) your family will be encouraged that growth is occurring. When your diligence and patience are waning, these hope-inducing observations of growth will be vital—for everyone. You may note the growth to them, journal their growth, share the growth to believers around you (e.g., your local church), or even commemorate the growth with a special celebration with specific thanksgiving to the Lord. A redemptive posture sees how growth is occurring and ensures to take note.

OWNING RESPONSIBILITIES

Almost the entire book is written towards those who are ministering to a loved one or counselee with PTSD; that is very intentional. Yet this last section of this chapter needs to shift gears for a moment to those who are suffering with PTSD.[7] In the most transparent and graceful way that I can muster, these next sentences are a charge and an encouragement. But before those are issued, it must be said that your pain, your suffering, your frustration and hurt are very real to all of us. We get it, really we do. We see what you are going through and wish at some level, that we could inherit that pain from you so that you did not have to bear it anymore. That is

---

7. I intend this section as a simple means of inducing the one suffering with PTSD to grow and be ready to change. Therefore, this section could simply be employed as a letter, call, invitation or any other means of bringing about this inducement.

why this book exists; that is why your loved one has read this book. We want to minister to you in a way that is helpful and biblical, or more accurately: biblically helpful.

In order to help you therefore, I charge you to submit yourself to them. They are not seeking anything other than your growth. They don't want what is yours, they want you (2 Cor 12:14). In a very real sense, they want your suffering to be gone as much as you do, perhaps even more. Will you submit to them? Will you place yourself under their authority? This process will be next to impossible if you are not going to submit to them or others in similar positions. You need the help, they want to help; will you let them? I pray your answer is a resounding, "Yes!"

An outworking of this submission to help is that you must recognize that you do need help. What you have experienced is terrible and to shoulder the burden of PTSD alone will be almost unbearable. Recognize that you need help, not in a sterile, call this toll free hotline capacity but help from real people who really love you. And, in some way, want the old you back. Do not let your own haughtiness prevent you from recognizing that you need help. Remember, it is the humble who receive grace (Jam 4:6).

Yet, you might be thinking: "They do not know what I went through, they were not there." Can I agree with you for a moment? You are right; they *were* not there. And maybe they have pretty tidy lives compared to what you have experienced. But let me ask you a question: would you really want them to have been there? Would you want that trauma to be experienced by anyone else? I think if you are totally transparent and honest you would say that you would not want anyone to go through what you have experienced. Moreover, to keep up this guarded mentality of "how could you know" is a mild form of pride. Pride says, "You don't know, therefore you cannot help me." Whereas humility recognizes that there is truly nothing new under the sun, including your suffering. The question is, "even if we were to usher in survivors from the Holocaust, would that really open your ears to listen?" Probably not. You must be willing to submit to people who may not have been there with you but can empathize with what you are experiencing.

Yes, your suffering was brutal, but do not hold it closer than you hold your family—the one's God has given to *you*. Do not fall into the trap of suffering elitism and comparing your suffering with others because, truth be told, in all of history there has only been one true Victim and it was not you or me: it was the God-man who laid down his life, his perfect life.

This does not defang the pain of your suffering but does exactly what it should; it contextualizes your suffering. It shows you that change is possible and growth is possible because if you are a child of God, he is at work in you (Phil 1:6) through the means of other people. In addition, this contextualization also says, "You need to work out your salvation—still" (Phil 2:12–13). You still have a responsibility to honor God in the middle of this mess and in order to grow, you have to take ownership of this responsibility.

And finally, PTSD is not the determining factor of your life and your future. I pray you find your identity in Christ and not in your suffering (Col 3:3). Do not let the VA, your counselor, the medical doctor, or even your peers convince you otherwise. You are a new creature who is in Christ if you are a believer in him and that should be your identity, not PTSD. Do not fall into the trap of letting your suffering or "disorder" be your identity because that is not accurate and to believe it is accurate will stymie your growth. Rather, identify PTSD as a weakness with which you struggle not a banner under which you fall. At the moment you believe PTSD to be who you are, you will find yourself to be right and this should terrify you.

Chapter 10

Conclusion

In a television broadcast, a popular televangelist sought to address the very issue of PTSD on Veteran's Day. In the broadcast, Kenneth Copeland read a passage from Numbers 32:20–22 very triumphantly and then pronounced what he (most likely) believed to be the liberating thought that those with PTSD needed to hear. "'You listen to me,' Copeland said, addressing the camera, 'you get rid of that right now. You don't take drugs to get rid of it, it doesn't take psychology; that promise right there [in Scripture] will get rid of it.'"[1] Much to his chagrin—and increased marginalization—Mr. Copeland has done exactly what I hope to avoid: he has over-simplified the complexities of PTSD.

If you, as the reader, have come away with anything from this book it should be a heightened awareness of the complexities of PTSD and the Scripture's robust ability to speak into those complexities. From that vein, I anticipate that your family will serve as the ministry context that your loved one needs. In the most robust way possible, your family is the context for ministry. The problem that authors like Mr. Copeland often embody is representing evangelicals to be simplistic individuals. Representing us to offer a "You get rid of that right now" mentality. May this work serve to bless people by understanding their complexities, not over-simplifying their complexities!

1. Benen, "This Week in God."

82

However, without fail there will be those who will mock your ministry to your family member suffering with PTSD. They will lump you into a naïve and borderline ignorant position similar to that of Mr. Copeland. They will hear that you believe the Bible to be true and helpful and automatically think you are going to provide some type of, "you get rid of it right now" advice. Do not be intimidated. As savvy as secular psychologies want to pose themselves to be, do not capitulate to their seemingly sophisticated views and treatments of PTSD. The Bible is truth and the measure of truth (John 17:17). Let it speak cogently into your loved one's life, not the traditions of man. Because you believe this does not make you naïve, it makes you counter-cultural!

Our culture will tell you that PTSD is a problem that Scripture does not articulate, but please remember that even though it doesn't use the term, it addresses the nature of PTSD. If you do not believe the Scriptures are sufficient to address the complexities of man's problems then you too will think that anything outside of secular psychology will sound Copeland-esque. If you do believe that the Creator of man has answers into created mans complex life, then I anticipate this to be a work that will be relevant and fresh to your personal ministry.

It is also my wish that this work will serve as a means of restoring a biblical worldview to those who are struggling with PTSD. As I have come to a conclusion of this work after studying PTSD for over five years, it has become apparent that much still needs to be done in this regard. This worldview needs fleshed-out in many ways but traction is being gained and progress is being made. PTSD will be the new ADD and we must think well about its newfound presence in our culture. And if you can say that this work has bolstered your thinking about PTSD and confidence in the power of God to change people, then success for me lies therein. "Now to him who is able to do far more abundantly than all that we ask or think, according to the power at work within us, to him be glory in the church and in Christ Jesus throughout all generations, forever and ever. Amen" (Eph 3:20–21).

Bibliography

Adams, Jay E. *A Theology of Christian Counseling: More than Redemption.* Grand Rapids: Zondervan, 1979.

———. *The Christian Counselor's Manual: The Practice of Nouthetic Counseling.* Grand Rapids: Zondervan, 1973.

Alcorn, Randy. *The Grace and Truth Paradox: Responding in Christlike Balance* Sisters, OR: Multnomah, 2003.

American Psychological Association, "Trauma" accessed April 6, 2017, http://www.apa.org/topics/trauma.

Arndt, William, Frederick W. Danker, and Walter Bauer. *A Greek-English Lexicon of the New Testament and Other Early Christian Literature,* 3rd ed. Chicago: University of Chicago, 2000. Electronic edition.

Athanasius. *De Synodis.* NewAdvent.org 359 AD. http://www.newadvent.org/fathers/2817.htm (accessed March 12, 2013).

Baxter, Richard. "The Cure of Melancholy and Overmuch Sorrow, by Faith." Fire and Ice Sermon Series. http://puritansermons.com (accessed November 1, 2012).

Benen, Steve. "This Week in God." MSNBC.com. November 16, 2013, http://www.msnbc.com/rachel-maddow-show/week-god-82 (accessed November 18, 2013).

Berg, Jim. "Understanding Biblical Change" in *Changed Into His Image: God's Plan for Transforming Your Life.* Greenville, SC: Bob Jones University, 1999.

Bridges, Jerry. *Who Am I? Identity in Christ.* Adelphi, MD: Cruciform, 2012.

Carson, D. A. *The Gospel According to John.* The Pillar New Testament Commentary. Grand Rapids, MI: Inter-Varsity; W.B. Eerdmans, 1991.

———. "The Function of the Paraclete in John 16:7–11" *Journal of Biblical Languages* 98/4 (1979) 547–566.

Chen, Yung. "Traumatic Stress and Religion: Is there a Relationship? A Review of Empirical Findings." *Journal of Religion and Health* 45 no. 3 (Fall 2006) 375–76.

Davids, Peter H. *The Letters of 2 Peter and Jude.* The Pillar New Testament Commentary. Grand Rapids, MI: William B. Eerdmans, 2006.

Eareckson Tada, Joni and Steve Estes. *When God Weeps: Why Our Sufferings Matter to the Almighty.* Grand Rapids: Zondervan, 1997.

Easton, M. G. *Easton's Bible Dictionary.* Oak Harbor, WA: Logos Research Systems, 1996. Electronic edition.

Eide, Arne. *Disability and Poverty: A Global Challenge.* Bristol: The Policy Press, 2011.

Fahlbusch, Erwin and Geoffrey William Bromiley. *The Encyclopedia of Christianity.* Grand Rapids, MI: Eerdmans, 1999–2003. S.v. "hope"; electronic edition.

Fettke, Tom ed. *The Celebration Hymnal: Songs and Hymns for Worship* (n.p.: Word Music Integrity Music, 1997.

Freedman, David Noel, Allen C. Myers and Astrid B. Beck. *Eerdmans Dictionary of the Bible.* Grand Rapids, MI: W.B. Eerdmans, 2000. S.v. "hope."

Friedmen, Mathew. "PTSD History and Overview," The Department of Veteran's Affairs. http://www.ptsd.va.gov/professional/pages/ptsd-overview.asp (accessed October 6, 2013).

Gesenius, Wilhelm and Samuel Prideaux Tregelles. *Gesenius' Hebrew and Chaldee Lexicon to the Old Testament Scriptures.* Bellingham, WA: Logos Bible Software, 2003. Electronic edition.

Grudem, Wayne. *Systematic Theology: An Introduction to Biblical Doctrine.* Grand Rapids: Zondervan, 1994.

Hart, Archibald D. *Counseling the Depressed* Vol. 5. Waco, TX: Word Books, 1987.

Hempy Jr., Robert E. "The Sufficiency of Scripture and Modern Psychology." *Chafer Theological Seminary Journal* Vol. 4 (January 1998) 10–13.

Hodges, Charles. Personal Correspondence: E-mail. May 16, 2013.

Jamison, Kay. *The Unquiet Mind: A Memoir of Moods and Madness.* New York, NY: Random House, 2009.

Kellemen, Robert. *God's Healing for Life's Losses: How to Find Hope When You Are Hurting.* Winona Lake, IN: BMH, 2010.

Kittel, Gerhard, Geoffrey W. Bromiley, and Gerhard Friedrich, eds. *Theological Dictionary of the New Testament.* Grand Rapids, MI: Eerdmans, 1964.

Lane, Tim. *PTSD: Healing for Bad Memories.* Greensboro, NC: New Growth Press, 2012.

Lea, Thomas D. and Hayne P. Griffin. *1, 2 Timothy, Titus.* The New American Commentary Vol. 34. Nashville: Broadman & Holman, 1992. Electronic edition.

Lloyd-Jones, D. Martin. *Spiritual Depression: Its Causes and Cures.* Grand Rapids: Eerdman's, 1965.

MacArthur Jr., John F. "The Sufficiency of Scripture," *The Master's Seminary Journal* 15/2 (Fall 2004) 165–174.

———. *The MacArthur Study Bible*. Nashville: Thomas Nelson, 1997.

Mack, Wayne A. "The Sufficiency of Scripture in Counseling," *The Master's Seminary Journal* 9:1 (Spring 1998) 64.

———. *A Homework Manual for Biblical Living*. Phillipsburg, NJ: P&R, 1979.

Marsella, Anthony. "Ethnocultural Aspects of PTSD: An Overview of Concepts, Issues, and Treatments." *Traumatology* 16 (4) 17–24.

Mathison, Keith A. *The Shape of Sola Scriptura*. Moscow, ID: Canon, 2001.

Meisinger, George. "The Sufficiency of Scripture for Life and Godliness: 2 Peter 1:1–4." *Chafer Theological Seminary Journal* 1:2 (Summer 1995) 5–10.

Mounce, William D. *Word Biblical Commentary: Pastoral Epistles*. Nashville: Thomas Nelson, 2000.

Muller, Robert. "Culture & PTSD: Lessons from the 2004 Tsunami." Psychology Today http://www.psychologytoday.com/blog/talking-about-trauma/201310/culture-ptsd-lessons-the-2004-tsunami (accessed October 8, 2013).

Murray, Caroline. "9 Sneaky Causes of Depression." Fox News. http://www.foxnews.com/health/2011/08/16/sneaky-causes-depression (accessed November 1, 2012).

New York Daily News. "New Psychiatric Manual, DSM-5, Faces Criticism for Turning 'Normal' Human Problems Into Mental Illness." New York Daily News http://www.nydailynews.com/life-style/health/shrinks-critics-face-new-psychiatric-manual-article-1.1344935#ixzz2bA58XDZS (accessed August 5, 2013).

Ozer, Emily and Daniel Weiss. "Who Develops Posttraumatic Stress Disorder?" *Current Directions in Psychological Science* 13 no. 4 (2004) 169–72.

Piper, John. "Abortion and the Narrow Way that Leads to Life." Desiring God. http://www.desiringgod.org/resource-library/sermons/abortion-and-the-narrow-way-that-leads-to-life (accessed September 6, 2013).

———. "Thoughts on the Sufficiency of Scripture," Desiring God http://www.desiringgod.org/resource-library/taste-see-articles/thoughts-on-the-sufficiency-of-scripture (accessed March 11, 2013).

Piper, John. *When the Darkness Will Not Lift*. Wheaton, IL: Crossway, 2006.

Rogers Jr., Cleon L. and Cleon Rogers III. *The New Linguistic and Exegetical Key to the Greek New Testament*. Grand Rapids: Zondervan, 1998.

Sage Publications. "What is Trauma?" Sage. http://www.sagepub.com/upm-data/11559_Chapter_1.pdf (accessed October 7, 2013).

Sande, Ken. *The Peace Maker: A Biblical Guide to Resolving Personal Conflict*. 1991; repr., Grand Rapids: Baker, 2004.

Schreiner, Thomas R. *1, 2 Peter, Jude*. The New American Commentary Vol. 37. Nashville: Broadman & Holman, 2003.

Scott, Stuart and Heath Lambert, eds. *Counseling the Hard Cases: True Stories Illustrating the Sufficiency of God's Resource in Scripture*. Nashville: B&H Academic, 2012.

———. "Biblical Hope in Discouragement Part 1." Sermon, Winnetka, CA: Come, Let Us Reason Together (accessed October 2012).

Shepherd, Rupert. "Post-traumatic Stress Disorder Linked to Genetics." Medical News Today. http://www.medicalnewstoday.com/articles/243717.php (accessed October 9, 2013).

Sibbes, Richard. *The Bruised Reed*. Carlisle, PA: Banner of Truth, 2005.

Smith, Robert. "A Physician Looks at Counseling: Depression." *The Journal of Biblical Counseling* 1 (1977) 85–88.

Strange, Dan. "Not Ashamed! The Sufficiency of Scripture for Public Theology," *Themelios* Vol. 36:2 (2011): 238–60.

The National Institute of Mental Health. "PTSD and Depression Epidemic Among Cambodian Immigrants." http://www.nimh.nih.gov/news/science-news/2005/ptsd-depression-epidemic-among-cambodian-immigrants.shtml (accessed July 13, 2013).

———. "What is Post-traumatic Stress Disorder?" http://www.nimh.nih.gov/health/topics/post-traumatic-stress-disorder-ptsd/index.shtml (accessed September 26, 2013).

The United States Department of Veteran's Affairs. "DSM-5 Criteria for PTSD." https://www.ptsd.va.gov/professional/PTSD-overview/dsm5_criteria_ptsd.asp.

Tietz, Peggy Kruger. "Emotions After Divorce." The Huffington Post http://www.huffingtonpost.com/dr-peggy-kruger-tietz/emotions-after-divorce_b_3575565.html (accessed November 1, 2013).

Tripp, Paul. *Instruments in the Redeemer's Hands: People in Need of Change Helping People in Need of Change*. Phillipsburg, NJ: P&R, 2002.

United States Department of Veterans Affairs. "DSM 5 Criteria for PTSD." http://www.ptsd.va.gov/professional/pages/dsm5_criteria_ptsd.asp (accessed August 4, 2013).

Warfield, B. B. *The Inspiration and Authority of the Bible*. Philadelphia: P&R, 1948.

Weeks, Noel. *The Sufficiency of Scripture*. Carlisle, PA: Banner of Truth Trust, 1988.

Welch, Ed. "Words of Hope for Those Who Struggle with Depression." *The Journal of Biblical Counseling* 18, no. 2 (Winter 2000) 45.

———. *Blame it on the Brain*. Philipsburg, NJ: P&R, 1998.

Young, Allan. *Harmony of Illusions: Inventing Post-Traumatic Stress Disorder*. Princeton, NJ: Princeton University, 1997.

Zimmerli, Walther. *Man and His Hope in the Old Testament*. London: SCM, 1971.

Made in the USA
Coppell, TX
05 February 2021